University of Washington Publications in Language and Literature
Volume XVII

Bibliography of Chaucer

1954-63

By William R. Crawford

UNIVERSITY OF WASHINGTON PRESS

Seattle and London

Copyright © 1967 by the University of Washington Press
Library of Congress catalogue card number 66-29836
Printed in the United States of America

For Geoffrey and Dudley

Vultures infernal
Tearing internal
Poets eternal
    and so on and so on.

—Dorothy Wellesley to W. B. Yeats

PREFACE

The division of this Bibliography into sections follows--with minor exceptions--the organization of D. D. Griffith's Bibliography of Chaucer, 1908-1953. Each section is keyed to the corresponding section in Griffith, and numerous page references to Griffith occur in the brief notes that often follow individual entries. Reprints and revised editions of Griffith items are noticed, and a number of Griffith entries are reproduced with additional information, such as reviews that appeared after 1953, appended. I have departed from Griffith's practice of listing YWES reviews because the widespread availability of this indispensable research tool renders such listing supererogatory.

My task as compiler has been made easier by the introduction in 1957 of international coverage in the annual MLA Bibliography, as well as by the high standards of excellence maintained by the bibliographical guides listed in the first section of this volume. I am particularly indebted to Thomas A. Kirby, chairman of the Committee on Research and Bibliography of the Chaucer Group of the Modern Language Association of America, who--together with his coeditors-- has for many years now compiled the reports of this committee. I have frequently consulted these reports, always with profit.

I should also like to acknowledge my indebtedness to Miss Virginia Close and her staff in the Reference Room of

Baker Library, Hanover, New Hampshire. Miss Close's expert knowledge has proved invaluable to me on more than one occasion. Funds for the typing of this manuscript have been made available to me by Dartmouth College through the Faculty Committee on Research. For the financial support of this institution, I am deeply grateful.

August, 1966
Dartmouth College
Boston University

CONTENTS

INTRODUCTION
NEW DIRECTIONS IN CHAUCER CRITICISM

This first supplement to D. D. Griffith's Bibliography of
Chaucer, 1908-1953, contains the cumulative record of
Chaucer scholarship and criticism produced in the ten-year
period from 1954 to 1963. Although I have not undertaken a
quantitative comparison of this volume with Griffith's, it
seems evident that the number of entries recorded for this
ten-year period is substantially larger than the total recorded for any similar period by Griffith or, for that matter,
by Eleanor Prescott Hammond. This productivity is one in-
dication of the continuing vitality of Chaucer studies; more
to the point, perhaps, is the observation that Chaucer's
poetry is of such a magnitude that the problems raised by
this poetry cannot simply be brushed aside and ignored.
Chaucer remains an insistent presence in English poetry
who demands, as does Shakespeare, to be understood by
each generation of readers. How he is understood in our
own time, an age characterized by re-examination of traditional moral, social, and literary values, is the subject
of this Introduction. I have selected for extensive discussion
in this essay a number of critical works which I believe to
be central to a modern re-evaluation of Chaucer's poetic
achievement. Examination of these works reveals significant new directions in recent Chaucer criticism. If this
introductory essay identifies several of these new

directions, it will have fulfilled one of its purposes. If it provokes further discussion of the means and ends of Chaucer criticism, it will have fulfilled an even larger purpose.

The body of Chaucer criticism produced in the last ten or twelve years is rich and varied. The questions being asked about Chaucer's poetry are significant ones, and the answers to these questions, if not always satisfying, at least point toward an emerging criticism of Chaucer which is distinctively modern. In the most general terms this criticism is concerned with defining Chaucer's poetic; that is, with the style or styles of individual poems and with the relationship of these styles to one or more of the great traditions that inform late medieval culture.

This search for a poetic that will serve as an adequate theoretical basis for criticism is, in large part, a reaction against the simplistic views of poetry, but especially of medieval poetry, held by an earlier generation of great Chaucerians. These earlier critics, important as their contribution to Chaucer scholarship may finally prove to have been, read Chaucer as a poet pre-eminent in the art of social and psychological realism. [1] The following sentence drawn from J. M. Manly's famous Warton Lecture of 1926 shows the force and direction of a cluster of largely unexamined, because seemingly self-evident, assumptions about Chaucer's art: "To any student of his technique, Chaucer's development reveals itself unmistakably . . . as a process of gradual release from the astonishingly artificial and sophisticated art with which he began and the gradual replacement of formal rhetorical devices by methods of composition based upon close observation of life and the exercise of the creative imagination. "[2] The first assumption

---

[1]For a lively critique of this earlier "official" view of Chaucer, with numerous references to Lowes, Root, Legouis, et al., see Wayne Shumaker, "Alisoun in Wander-land: A Study in Chaucer's Mind and Literary Method, " ELH, 18, 1951, 77-89 (Griffith, p. 77).
[2]"Chaucer and the Rhetoricians, " Proceedings of the

underlying this sentence is that Chaucer's "development" as an artist lay in one direction only; the second is that this development can best be seen as "a process of gradual release" from traditional medieval poetic art; and, finally, it is assumed that Chaucer emerged from the bondage of a traditional (and "astonishingly artificial") art into the freedom of a vaguely romantic poetic "based upon close observation of life and the exercise of the creative imagination."

Now if these assumptions about Chaucer's art are accepted uncritically, and they have been, then a special kind of criticism will inevitably result. The poet will be valued more highly for his "observations" of human nature (his psychological insight into character) than for his ability to make character serve the interest of a larger narrative design. The endless discussions about the "character flaw" of Criseyde and the equally endless debate about the relative merits of Palamon and Arcite in the "Knight's Tale" are both examples of a fundamental confusion about the nature of "art" in relation to "observed life." When the critic is faced, as he is in the "Clerk's Tale," with a poem in which there is no observable connection between literary character and psychological reality, he is forced to condemn the story in which the characters appear as "in no way consonant with the truth of life."[3]

British Academy, 12, 1926, 97 (Griffith, p. 123). Charles Muscatine quotes the same sentence on p. 174 of Chaucer and the French Tradition: A Study in Style and Meaning (see below, pp. 24-25) and adds the following comment: "The contention that Chaucer gradually abandoned rhetoric is statistically questionable. More questionable yet is the assumption that rhetoric is automatically bad. It takes only a little reflection to see that the use of forms which the critic can describe as rhetorical is one of the principal characteristics of poetry."

[3]This quotation from Lounsbury is cited by James Sledd in "The Clerk's Tale: The Monsters and the Critics," MP, 51, 1953, 73-82 (Griffith, p. 213). Professor Sledd writes (on p. 75): " . . . the assumptions of the standards of

A similar confusion about the relationship of "art" to
"observed life" is at the root of yet another controversy
with which, in the past, Chaucer criticism has been encum-
bered. I am thinking of the vast amount of writing in which
the critic assumes that the doctrine of "Courtly Love" is a
historical phenomenon as well documented in the annals of
the Middle Ages as is the Black Death. Once this assumption is made, poems that are shaped in part by a set of conventions proper to the genre of romance come to be seen as
problems in social criticism, and Chaucer almost inevitably
emerges from the discussion, as he does in The Allegory
of Love, as a prophet of social melioration. E. Talbot
Donaldson has recently written that "such a definition of
courtly love as C. S. Lewis' seems to be the result of a
confusion on his part of literary criticism with supposedly
objective historical facts which he derived mainly from the
earlier literature he was examining."[4] Awareness of the

---

realistic fiction makes possible [in the "Clerk's Tale"] the
initial assertion that the story is peculiar, contradictory,
and irrational." For discussions of Criseyde's character as
a part of the larger design of Troilus and Criseyde, I refer
the reader to the following: Arthur Mizener, "Character and
Action in the Case of Criseyde," PMLA, 54, 1939, 65-81
(Griffith, p. 304); Sanford B. Meech, Design in Chaucer's
Troilus (see below, p. 100), especially chap. iii, "Figura-
tive Associations in Seven Areas"; Charles Muscatine,
Chaucer and the French Tradition, chap. v; and Robert O.
Payne, The Key of Remembrance (see below, p. 25) espe-
cially chap. vi.

[4]This sentence is quoted from an article entitled "The
Myth of Courtly Love," which appeared in a recent issue
(Fall, 1965) of Ventures: Magazine of the Yale Graduate
School, pp. 16-23. Donaldson's argument is in part sup-
ported by the historical investigations of J. F. Benton,
"The Court of Champagne as a Literary Center" (see below,
p. 110). D. W. Robertson, Jr., has likewise questioned,
on other grounds, the assumptions made by Lewis and
others that "Courts of Love" actually flourished in the

circular reasoning implied by such an assumption has enabled the modern critic to concentrate on literary rather
than on social problems. The critic is freed to ask the same
question about literary convention that he is able to ask
about character: What use does Chaucer make of this body
of conventions in the larger design of the poem? More important, he is able to ask an even more central question: In
what way do these conventions give rise to stylistic varia-
tion within the works of one poet, or even within the limits
of a single poem?

From one point of view it may be argued that, while the
critics we have been discussing have indeed challenged the
assumptions upon which an earlier body of Chaucer criticism
was based, they have succeeded only in substituting for one
set of outmoded assumptions about Chaucer's art another
set more congenial to that illusive wraith, the "modern tem-
per." According to this view, urged most forcefully by
D. W. Robertson, Jr., and Bernard Huppé, Chaucer has
not so much been read anew by critics such as Donaldson,
Muscatine, and Payne (to cite three critics whose works
will be examined in some detail in this essay) as he has
been recreated in a modern, and therefore uncongenial,
idiom. Because medieval poetry is essentially different
from modern poetry, critical tools forged in the workshop
of twentieth-century criticism will, according to Professor
Robertson's view, yield all the wrong results when applied

Middle Ages; see A Preface to Chaucer (below, p. 26), especially chap. v, "Some Medieval Doctrines of Love." See
also in this connection the Introduction (pp. 7 ff.) to D. S.
Brewer's edition of The Parlement of Foulys (below, pp.
93-94), and James J. Wilhelm, The Cruelest Month (New
Haven, Conn.: Yale University Press, 1965). On p. 165
Wilhelm notes: "It is sadly ironic that, despite the tomes
written about courtly love and the adoration of women in
twelfth-century France, history furnishes no convincing
proofs to support the cultural generalizations based on poetic fiction. Possibly the conceit is merely witty."

to poetry written nearly six hundred years ago.[5]

Professor Robertson proposes as an alternative to modern criticism an enlightened historicism which attempts first to recover and then to assimilate the medieval poetic, and finally to interpret Chaucer's poetry solely in the light of this poetic. Central to this neo-Augustinian poetic is the tenet that all art (including the art of poetry) is ultimately concerned with promoting the doctrine of caritas, either directly or by an ironic overpraising of cupiditas. The modern reader is able to penetrate the sometimes deliberately deceptive surface (cortex) of a medieval poem and apprehend its central core of meaning (sententia) only by applying to a study of that poem the techniques that enabled the medieval exegete to interpret the mysteries of scriptural allegory. Only by these means can the values in Chaucer's poetry which are essentially medieval, and which therefore distinguish this poetry from modern poetry, be recovered. I am not concerned here with the success, to date, of this enterprise, but only with pointing out that such an undertaking involves jettisoning as irrelevant baggage the habits of mind accumulated--according to Robertson's reckoning--during the last two hundred years. The attempt is no doubt a noble one; it remains to be seen whether or not it is also a possible one.

When the spectrum of recent interpretive studies of Chaucer's poetry is surveyed, even in so brief and fragmentary a fashion as this, a distinctive pattern emerges. A modern criticism has challenged the assumptions of an older historicism based largely upon late romantic assumptions

---

[5]Cf. A Preface to Chaucer, p. 9: "The various aesthetic systems that have arisen since art became an entity in itself have a valid application to post-romantic art and literature, but they have little relevance to the art and literature of the pre-romantic past. " In a note to the sentence preceding the one quoted here, Professor Robertson writes: "It is probable that the really decisive break in the European tradition should be placed in the last half of the eighteenth century rather than in the Renaissance. "

about the nature of poetry. A new historicism has, in its
turn, challenged the assumptions of both the older historicism and the new criticism. The new critics have joined
the issue with enthusiasm, pointing with the fervor of an
evangelical missionary to the text as the court of final authority. [6] This procedure has in turn been dismissed as a
too "literal" reading of the text; that is, the latent symbol-
ogy of the text is available only to those who have trained
themselves to read the text through the eyes of a medieval
exegete. [7]

Before examining in greater detail several works which,
to my mind, have made significant contributions to modern
Chaucer criticism, it might prove helpful for us to step
back from the fray and identify those areas of agreement
shared by practitioners both of the new criticism and of the
new historicism. Neither group of critics entertains doubts
about the seriousness or worth of Chaucer's poetry, even if
what is found to be of value by one group is discarded as
"chaf" by the other. This implicit judgment of the magnitude
of Chaucer's poetry has forced critics of whatever persua-
sion to respond to the need to formulate a poetic adequate
to the demands of interpretive criticism, no matter how
broadly "interpretive criticism" must be defined within this

---

[6]This position is succinctly stated by Talbot Donaldson in
his Preface (p. vi) to Chaucer's Poetry (see below, p. 12):
"The fact that the difference between what these two historical approaches have attained is absolute--if Chaucer means
what the older Chaucerians thought he meant he cannot possibly mean what these newer Chaucerians think he means--
has encouraged me to rely on the poems as the principal
source of their meaning."

[7]Cf. Robertson, A Preface to Chaucer, p. 287: "Even
more important, perhaps, as a deterrent to our appreciation of allegory is the fact that its presence cannot be de-
tected by modern philological methods. Scientific scholarship insists on confining itself to what a text 'actually says.'
During the Middle Ages, this restriction was sometimes
regarded not as a virtue but as a mark of illiteracy."

particular context. The initial steps in the formulation of
such a poetic have meant for the critic a re-examination of
Chaucer's language, conventional themes, and poetic
styles, and a reformulation of the relationship of the poems
that embody these characteristics to the cross currents of
late Gothic culture. [8]

Modern Chaucer criticism can be traced to no one semi-
nal book and to no single critic. It is rather the expression
of a felt need to deliver Chaucer from a limbo peopled by
virtuous poets whose importance is primarily historical.
The first two book-length studies to bear this distinctively
modern imprint are John Speirs's Chaucer the Maker (1951)
and Raymond Preston's Chaucer (1952). [9] These two books
share in many of the same virtues as well as in many of the
same defects. Both are admittedly--to use the words which
turn up frequently in reviews of the two books--"crotchety"
and "scrappy, " by which the reviewer means, particularly
in the case of Speirs, insistently nonacademic. A more serious fault with which both books can be taxed is that quotation of Chaucer's verse is frequently substituted for criticism of that verse; in Preston's Chaucer, for example, over
750 lines from Chaucer alone are quoted in the first 4 chapters (71 pages). Both books in fact deliver less than they
promise, and the slack is taken up not only by quotation but
(with Speirs) by fulmination against "pedantry" and (in Preston's book) by epigram and distant allusion. In both books

---

[8]Cf. the review article by Charles Muscatine entitled
"Chaucer in an Age of Criticism, " MLQ, 25, 1964, 473-78,
especially the discussion (pp. 474-75) of Wolfgang Clemen's
Chaucer's Early Poetry (see below, p. 20) for a similar
statement of new directions in Chaucer criticism. I am indebted to this review article, as well as to other works by
Muscatine, for many of the ideas developed in this Introduction.
[9]John Speirs, Chaucer the Maker (London: Farrar and
Faber, 1951); see Griffith, p. 77. Raymond Preston, Chaucer (New York: Sheed and Ward, 1952); see Griffith, p. 75.

impressionistic statements abound, particularly about language. This is more painfully true of Speirs that of Preston, because Speirs venerates the English language as the
vehicle of the "Great Tradition."[10]

These faults, and others, have more than adequately been
pointed out in reviews of the two books. What has been less
emphatically demonstrated is that both books are concerned
(in no matter how halting a fashion) with Chaucer's <u>poetry</u>,
even when the critical tools employed to get at that poetry
have proved inadequate. Both critics are convinced of the
value of Chaucer's poetry from the admittedly limited perspective of the mid-twentieth century; thus they have avoid-
ed the implications of a historical compartmentalization
which has crippled so much post-Victorian criticism of
Chaucer.[11] The "value" which both Speirs and Preston have
discovered--or, more properly, "rediscovered"--in Chaucer's poetry is quite simply the value of complexity. Preston writes, with immediate reference to the <u>Parliament of
Birds</u>, that "without distorting his lucid diction, Chaucer
has written with a complexity that makes the complication
of most verse today appear a child's puzzle" (p. 44). With
this statement compare Speirs (p. 204): "The 'simplicity'
of Chaucer's poetry is in fact complex and genuinely sophisticated by comparison with modern complicatedness the
pretenses of which often go under the name of 'sophistica-
tion.'"

At this point an important distinction must be made. For
Speirs, Chaucer's poetic complexity is a reflection of the
"mediaeval English organic community" which is implied in
that poetry. "It is a community dissociated neither from
nature nor from its past. The specifically Christian carols

---

[10]It is interesting to note in this connection that both
Speirs and Preston underestimate the difficulty of Middle
English for the modern reader.

[11]Cf. Payne, <u>The Key of Remembrance</u>, p. 3: "And certainly it is a self-contradictory historicism which labels
anachronistic a comparison of Chaucer and Eliot while sanc-
tioning one of Chaucer and Ovid."

can be shown to be rooted in pre-Christian fertility ritual
. . . " (p. 216). For Preston Chaucer remains "the great
ironist" who, in contrast to Shakespeare, "kept in reserve,
at a given point in his story, the completeness of the narrative and of possible attitudes towards it" (p. 104). Speirs is
the less trustworthy guide at this point because his explanation of Chaucer's complexity implies a Lawrentian mindless-
ness and instinctive response to a "lost harmony between
man and nature. "[12] Preston is surely on sounder grounds
when he attributes Chaucer's complexity to a skeptical cast
of mind possible only in "a society of developed religion"
(p. 56; see also p. 115).

This is one of the major themes of Preston's book, and it
is a theme with important implications for modern criticism.
Chaucer's way of telling a story from multiple perspectives
reflects a skeptical intelligence which is neither, in Preston's words, "unbelief nor frozen doubt. " "Chaucer has his
own way of examining the sides of a question: he will look at
them one by one, so that he can think of them all together.
It is not merely that, as I have said, Chaucer tells a story
with different layers. He tells it . . . from different points
of view" (p. 65). With this statement modern criticism of
Chaucer may be said to have had a beginning.

Not many pages of either book we have been considering
are devoted to what is called, in modern critical jargon, a
"close reading" of the text. By "close reading" I mean only
the detailed examination of the verbal texture of a given
work in order to discover its meaning, rather than an examination of the "content" of a literary work in order to be
able to relate that work to its background, whether historical, philosophical, biographical, or other. The problems
faced by the modern critic who would attempt "close reading"
of medieval literature in general or of Chaucer in particular

---

[12]See Speirs, p. 101, note 1 (continued on p. 102), and
especially p. 204, where he writes: "If [Chaucer] is not a
"moralist" as Dante is, his poetry is profoundly moral and
profoundly religious in a Lawrentian sense (if one thinks
again of the opening of the Canterbury Tales). "

have been cogently summarized in the first chapter of
A. C. Spearing's Criticism and Mediaeval Poetry: "Close
reading . . . clearly depends for its success on a delicate
response to fine shades of meaning and tone. We may find
that such a response comes naturally to us in reading the
writers of our own age, because their language is ours. . . .
But to achieve such a response towards literature even older than [Shakespeare's] seems almost impossibly difficult,
simply because of the language problem." [13]
    It is not surprising that one of the most consistently en-
lightening of the modern critics of Chaucer, E. Talbot
Donaldson, brings to a "close reading" of Chaucer's poetry
the disciplines of the "old-line" philologist and editor.
Donaldson's interpretive criticism, scattered widely through
journals and Festschriften and collected only in the "Commentary" to his edition of Chaucer, is, as one reviewer has
remarked, a deceptively simple ad hoc response to the text
before him. This critical response is "deceptively simple"
in part because Donaldson's prose, even when he is discussing complex matters of poetic strategy, remains lucid,
unpretentious, and witty. This criticism is also "deceptively
simple"--like the poetry which is its only subject--for a
related reason: that quality which Northrop Frye defined as
a "sense of tact." [14] A single sentence quoted from Donaldson's discussion of the portrait of the Knight in the General
Prologue will illustrate this "sense of tact" in operation:
"Indeed, when we are told that the Knight was 'full worthy
in his lord's war,' it almost seems as if we are to understand not his earthly overlord but God." [15] The observation
is made in the criticism with a force which is proportional

---

[13] (London: Edward Arnold, 1964), p. 6.
[14] Anatomy of Criticism (Princeton, N. J.: Princeton University Press, 1957), p. 86: "The sense of tact, of the de-
sirability of not pushing a point of interpretation 'too far,'
is derived from the fact that the proportioning of emphasis
in criticism should normally bear a rough analogy to the
proportioning of emphasis in the poem."
[15] "Commentary" to Chaucer's Poetry, p. 882.

to that with which the divine overtone of "lordes" is sounded, but not insisted upon, in the General Prologue. It is impossible, finally, to "account" for either style or tact in criticism; it is possible, however, to suggest that those difficulties noted by A. C. Spearing can at least be mitigated if the critic first masters the disciplines of philology and editorial procedure.

The article by Donaldson in which literary criticism of a high order is most obviously based upon linguistic analysis is entitled "Idiom of Popular Poetry in the Miller's Tale."[16] The important article by Margaret Schlauch entitled "Chaucer's Colloquial English: Its Structural Traits" should also be mentioned in connection with Donaldson's.[17] After analyzing various "linguistic structures" to be found in Chaucer's poetry, Miss Schlauch comments upon the appropriateness of these structures to the speakers' "characteristic ways of organizing experience." These two articles are milestones in the history of modern criticism because together they provide an operational definition of one extreme of Chaucer's stylistic range. In order to formulate the other extreme of Chaucer's style, the courtly or artificial, the critic is driven, as we shall see, to combine formal rhetorical analysis with linguistic. These two articles are, finally, important because they demonstrate a method which enables literary criticism to result directly from philological investigation; linguistic analysis of the text is turned inward in order that the critic may examine the poems as verbal constructs, rather than turned outward in order to identify the historical matrix in which a literary document is imbedded.

A second major contribution which Donaldson has made to modern Chaucer criticism is his skilled treatment of complex matters of poetic strategy, particularly his discussion of the narrative points of view from which Chaucer chooses to tell his stories. The observation that the "I" in the poems is an artistic fiction, and a fiction endemic to narrative poetry of all ages, rather than an autobiographical fact, did

---

[16]See Griffith, pp. 193-94, and below, p. 66.
[17]PMLA, 67, 1952, 1103-16 (Griffith, pp. 126 and 139).

not, of course, originate with Donaldson. As he notes in
the article entitled "Chaucer the Pilgrim, " Kittredge made
the same observation "in a page of great importance to
Chaucer criticism. "[18] What is original in this article is
Donaldson's precise characterization of the Pilgrim-
narrator of the Canterbury Tales and the equally precise
demonstration that this narrator is the "chief agent by
which the poet achieves his wonderfully complex, ironic,
comic, serious vision of the world . . ." (p. 929).

Donaldson's characterization of the Pilgrim-narrator,
his discussion of the artistic functions of this persona
within the fiction of the Canterbury Tales, and his statement
of the complex interplay between Chaucer-the-pilgrim and
Chaucer-the-poet, have provoked, as might be expected, a
wide range of responses. John M. Major, writing in PMLA,
agrees that "the Narrator of the General Prologue is a persona of some sort, " but denies that the narrator "invented"
by Donaldson conforms to the facts of the poem. [19] Major
discovers instead a narrator who is "a marvelously alert,

---

[18]See below, p. 63, for notice of original publication and
reprint of "Chaucer the Pilgrim." The substance of the
article is summarized in Donaldson's "Commentary" to
Chaucer's Poetry, pp. 877-81. The reference to Kittredge
is to his discussion of the assumed pose of naïveté of the
Narrator in the Book of the Duchess in Chaucer and His
Poetry (Cambridge, Mass.: Harvard University Press,
1915), pp. 45-53 (see Griffith, p. 68). The year before
Donaldson's article appeared, Ben Kimpel discussed the
same topic in an article entitled "The Narrator of the Can-
terbury Tales, " ELH, 20, 1953, 77-86 (Griffith, p. 156).
In contrast to Donaldson, Kimpel argues (p. 86) that "the
Narrator in the Canterbury Tales is not a definite enough
personality to prove anything. " Edgar Hill Duncan's essay
("Narrator's Points of View in the Portrait Sketches, Pro-
logue to the Canterbury Tales") appeared in 1954 in the
Curry Festschrift (see below, p. 63). Duncan's article and
Donaldson's are mutually independent.

[19]For Major's article, see below, p. 63.

ironic, facetious master of every situation . . . " (p. 162).
He is the "alter ego" of the poet.

Major's argument, which does not entirely escape the
time-honored confusion of verisimilitude with actuality, is
essentially this: If Chaucer had indeed created a narrative
persona like the one characterized by Donaldson, he would
have been guilty of artistic inconsistency or of gross prodi-
gality--or both--because the voice of the persona is used
only "intermittently" in the Canterbury Tales. A narrator
such as the one Donaldson describes, once he has been invented by Chaucer, must, so the argument runs, be "per-
mitted to do all of the narrating, and to do it in his own
style, as dictated by the kind of man he is" (p. 161), lest
the realistic framework of the poem be violated.

The net effect of telescoping Chaucer-the-Poet and
Chaucer-the-Pilgrim into a single alert, ironic master of
all situations is precisely as damaging to a reading of Chaucer's poetry as is the older confusion--which Kittredge was
at pains to straighten out--in which both poet and narrator
are regarded as naive simpletons; in each case the critic
discards the very instrument by which Chaucer first cre-
ates and then controls his irony.

If Major denies that the persona of the Canterbury Tales
exists as Donaldson has described him, Bertrand H. Bronson denies that a persona exists at all: "I have little hesita-
tion in saying that nine-tenths of this talk [about Chaucer's
persona] is misguided and palpably mistaken."[20] Bronson's
arguments are based largely upon historical evidence, or
rather upon an acknowledgment of a lack of certain kinds of
historical evidence ("We need more historical knowledge")
which would illuminate the relationship between a poet who
wrote for oral delivery and the audience before whom the
poems were performed.[21] Discussions of the persona in
Chaucer's poetry are consequently based upon assumptions

---

[20]In Search of Chaucer, p. 26 (see below, p. 19).
[21]Cf. Payne's comments (The Key of Remembrance,
pp. 132 et passim) on the use of a historical audience as a
"standard of critical judgment."

that are essentially anachronistic: "The world of print makes
possible things never dreamed of in Chaucer's philosophy
and we must not impute to him a state of mind that would
only develop in later eras" (p. 26). The line of reasoning is
familiar from criticism of Shakespeare which is similarly
oriented; the only counterargument that comes easily to mind
is that we will never know what one of Shakespeare's audi-
tors--much less one of Chaucer's--really thought about
what he was hearing. Perhaps nearer to the point, however,
is the observation that the etymology of the word persona,
together with its modern English derivative "impersonate, "
suggests that the concept did not originate with T. S. Eliot's
"Prufrock. "

Bronson's caveats are worth heeding, and the questions
he asks demand answering because they have behind them
the force of a healthy skepticism: "Can we honestly assure
ourselves that we understand Chaucer's mind and art if we
lack adequate understanding of his procedure in crucial and
climactic moments of his best work?" The question is so
central to the concerns of modern Chaucer criticism, and
so cogently phrased by Bronson, that I shall quote in full the
elaborative sentence that follows the question: "We are not
merely disturbed, we are sometimes disoriented and
amazed by the rapid shifts of stylistic level, the apparent
sacrifice of achieved effects, the reversals of mood and
tone, the abrupt stoppage of narrative momentum, the com-
mingling of colloquial and artificial diction, the breathtaking
incorporation of the whole range of language into the working
texture of the verse" (p. 22).

A partial answer to Bronson's question, but without direct
reference to it, is contained in Talbot Donaldson's essay,
"The Ending of Chaucer's Troilus. "[22] In this essay Donaldson traces the tortuous progress of the narrator of the Troilus through the last eighteen stanzas of the poem. This
essay combines analyses of linguistic structures (see especially pp. 40 ff.), of "rapid shifts in stylistic levels" (see
especially p. 36), and of "apparent sacrifice of achieved

---

[22]See below, p. 97.

effects" (see especially p. 39) in order to demonstrate that
"at the end of Troilus Chaucer has manipulated a narrator
capable of only a simple view of reality in such a way as to
achieve the poetic expression of an extraordinarily complex
one" (p. 43).

I have dealt at such length with Donaldson's discussion of
the persona in the General Prologue and in Troilus and
Criseyde because the distinction between narrator and poet
is a crucial one for modern criticism. Such a distinction is,
to quote once again from Northrop Frye, "the most elemen-
tary of all distinctions in literature, the distinction between
fiction and fact, hypothesis and assertion, imaginative and
discursive writing. . . ." Failure to make this distinction
produces, as Frye goes on to point out, "what in criticism
has been called the 'intentional fallacy.'"[23] That is, if the
narrator's obtuse failure "to save appearances" within the
poem is identified with Chaucer's own, then we invite ourselves to speculate about what Chaucer was obscurely aim-
ing at--without really hitting--in a poem. If, on the other
hand, we recognize that the narrator's vision from within
the poem is one of several partial views, manipulated by the
poet in order to multiply the perspectives from which the
action is presented, then we are in a better position to see
the poem as a complex, ironic whole.

The subject of the critical work which I wish to consider
next, Charles Muscatine's Chaucer and the French Tradition, is Chaucer's participation in "that international, Gothic tradition of which French is the central literature"
(p. 245).[24] Since "Gothic" is one of those capacious and
illusive terms in the critical lexicon that always just escape
precise definition, Muscatine is at some pains to identify,
by quoting from Arnold Hauser, that particular quality of

---

[23]Anatomy of Criticism, p. 86; see also the discussion by
W. K. Wimsatt, Jr., of "The Intentional Fallacy" in The
Verbal Icon: Studies of the Meaning of Poetry (Lexington,
Ky.: University of Kentucky Press, 1954).
   [24]See below, pp. 24-25.

the Gothic manner with which he is concerned: "The basic
form of Gothic art is juxtaposition. Whether the individual
work is made up of several comparatively independent parts
or is not analyzable into such parts, whether it is a pictorial or a plastic, an epic or a dramatic representation, it is
always the principle of expansion and not of concentration,
of co-ordination and not of subordination, of the open se-
quence and not of the closed geometric form, by which it is
dominated. "[25] In literature Gothic form is characterized by
the juxtaposition of two conventional styles, the "Courtly"
and the "Bourgeois. "[26] Although these styles can be traced,

---

[25]The quotation from Hauser's The Social History of Art
(New York: Alfred A. Knopf, 1952) appears on pp. 167-68
of Chaucer and the French Tradition. Compare, however,
the contradictory view expressed by Otto von Simson with
reference to the principles of "Gothic Form" as those principles were embodied in architecture (The Gothic Cathedral,
pp. 8 et passim): "It is no longer necessary to insist on the
overwhelming importance of this geometrical element in
Gothic design. It constitutes the very principle of its order
and aesthetic cohesion. " For notice of von Simson's book,
see below, pp. 129-30.
[26]This terminology, as Muscatine says (p. 70), follows
Joseph Bédier, Les Fabliaux, 5th ed. (Paris, 1928); in the
same year in which Chaucer and the French Tradition was
published (1957), Per Nykrog challenged Bédier's alignment
of literary style with social class. The effect of Nykrog's
book (Les Fabliaux; see below, pp. 46 and 106) is to
strengthen Muscatine's critical argument by eliminating the
necessity for having to account, on historical grounds, for
Bédier's formulation. Nykrog's thesis, quoted from p. xli,
is as follows: "Ici nous pouvons reprendre la formule qui
est le point de départ de la deuxième partie de l'étude de
Bédier, et dire: les aristocrates du XIIIe siècle sont
responsables des récits dont ils se sont amusés, même
s'ils ne les ont pas inventés. --La séparation opérée par
Bédier est donc, selon ses propres principes, sans intérêt

following Bédier, to origins in the aristocratic and commer-
cial classes of medieval France, they tend to become, with
the passage of time, "independent of historical association"
(p. 2). The "courtly" style--the style of the Romance--sup-
ports attitudes which are idealistic and which reflect the
"mediaeval aesthetic theory of beauty as formal excellence
and brightness" (p. 18). The "bourgeois" style--the style of
the fabliau--supports attitudes which are phenomenalistic
and which reflect the nominalist tradition of philosophy in
the Middle Ages. Neither style exists in a "pure" state:
"We have seen realism in romance, and fragments of romance in the bourgeois poems . . . " (p. 71). The mixture
of styles represents not confusion on the part of the poet,
but an expression in literature of the guiding principle of
Gothic art, the principle of juxtaposition. Jean de Meun's
continuation of the Roman de la Rose--a poem which "holds
the Courtly and the 'realistic' views, among others, in
something of an ordered opposition to each other" (p. 74)--
constitutes Chaucer's most immediate stylistic heritage.
Chaucer was to explore this heritage, tentatively at first in
the Book of the Duchess, the House of Fame, and the Parliament of Fowls, and later with complete mastery in Troilus and Criseyde and in the Canterbury Tales.
    So runs the historical argument of the book; the critical
theory by which Muscatine is able to direct this historical
argument toward criticism of Chaucer's poetry is a conse-
quence of the critic's conception of style and of his insight
into the relation of style to the total meaning of a given
poem. "By a style I mean a particular combination of literary traits, large or small; by a conventional style I mean
one that is relatively stable over a long period of time"
(p. 2). Neither conventional style, courtly or bourgeois, is
inherently superior to the other because each style, selec-
tively refined over a period of time, serves to express
certain well-defined but necessarily limited areas of meaning. By juxtaposition of these styles, a third area of complex

---

pour les textes qui nous sont parvenus. Et alors que reste-
t-il de la thèse du 'fabliau-genre bourgeois'?"

meanings is discovered which is greater than the sum of its
two parts. The selective opposition of these two styles in
the interest of ironic perspective is the particular mark of
Chaucer's most mature achievement.

A summary as bald as that which I have just given of
Chaucer and the French Tradition does no justice to the co-
gency with which Muscatine has worked out this historico-
critical position. It does serve to demonstrate that the area
of critical concern--style as a function of meaning--which
Muscatine has staked out in this book is complementary to
Donaldson's criticism. Both Muscatine and Donaldson are
concerned with complex matters of poetic strategy, not for
their own sake, but in the interest of recovering meaning,
and the conclusions of one critic often reinforce those of the
other. Thus Donaldson's discussion of Chaucer's manipulation of the narrator in Troilus and Criseyde suggests one
means by which Chaucer created a poem which is complex,
ironic, and coherent; Muscatine's discussion of Chaucer's
manipulation of his stylistic resources in Troilus and
Criseyde supports a view of the poem which is similar.
Like Donaldson, Muscatine never strays far from the text
of a poem; consequently his generalizations about style have
a solidity of detail behind them which carries conviction.
And, finally, neither critic pretends to have produced a
"definitive" criticism of Chaucer. [27] This disclaimer is
worth underscoring because it is not, in the case of either
critic, merely a polite expression of the topos of "affected
modesty" or an argument for critical relativism. Critical
self-consciousness produces in the best of our critics an

---

[27]Compare Donaldson, p. v of the Preface to Chaucer's
Poetry ("'Definitive' criticism of Chaucer is obviously an
impossibility") with Muscatine, p. 9 (The present study
"will show that variant, respectable interpretations of
Chaucer's poems often correspond to varying areas of his
style, and thus that besides serving to define shifts of sen-
sibility, variant interpretations are abstractions from the
total poem, are actually variant and partial discoveries of
meaning. ").

awareness of the limitations of the analytical tools with
which criticism necessarily is undertaken. A historically
oriented critic, whether of the older or of the newer persua-
sion, is rarely as aware that the answer to a particular
question is already partially present in the formulation of
the question.

Muscatine's study of Chaucer's poetry in relation to his
immediate stylistic heritage is a solid achievement in its
own right; it also lays open a vast area for future critical
investigation. Muscatine writes (on p. 5) that "Chaucer's
deepest linguistic matrix is English, but if his diction and
syntax were English before him, his style was not." The
most inviting area of critical concern which Muscatine has
helped to open up is the detailed investigation of Chaucer's
greatest technical accomplishment--the fine adjustment of
his English diction and syntax to the values of conventional
styles. Further exploration in this area will, as Muscatine
suggests, require on the part of the critic a heady union of
philological knowledge and sensitivity to stylistic nuance:
"A fully satisfactory study of the style of [the Canterbury
Tales] . . . would have to face the monumental problem of
the stylistic value of Chaucer's language per se" (p. 6). The
charge to the critic has been sounded most eloquently, perhaps, by F. W. Bateson; writing of the antithesis of styles
in Chaucer's poetry, Bateson draws this conclusion: "But--
except occasionally by such scholars as Margaret Schlauch
and Charles Muscatine--the opposition has not been worked
out systematically at the level of diction or metre. The
horse, as usual, has been overlooked in favour of the cart.
After all, narrative excellence and brilliance of realistic
characterization are only the effects: their cause is the
style."[28]

Recognition of limitations, of areas for future exploration,
in no way detracts from the solid contribution which Chaucer and the French Tradition has made to Chaucer studies.

---

[28]The quotation from Bateson is taken from an Editorial
Appendix which he supplied to an essay by D. S. Brewer;
for reference, see below, p. 43, under Brewer.

The book contains, in the first place, illuminating analyses
of individual poems within the Chaucer canon. Second, a
number of these analyses are the direct result of Muscatine's
reformulation of critical problems which have persisted in
Chaucer criticism, such as the meaning of character within
different stylistic conventions. A third contribution is Muscatine's insistence that style is a function of the total meaning of a poem, and is inseparable from that meaning. Fourth,
he has examined Chaucer's sources from a perspective
which avoids the limitations of a strictly generic view. [29]
And, finally, Chaucer's relationship to the crosscurrents
of late Gothic art has been explored anew in Chaucer and the
French Tradition. These topics run the gamut of literary
concerns, from "close reading" of the text to art history in
its most inclusive sense; all of us who attempt to compre-
hend Chaucer's poetic achievement are in Charles Muscatine's debt.

In the course of his discussion (in The Discarded Image)
of the Seven Liberal Arts, C. S. Lewis remarks that the
revival of interest in medieval rhetoric is "a welcome novelty in twentieth-century medievalism. "[30] This revival,

----

[29]Cf. the important critique of the "closed system of in
vacuo source studies" (the theory of "linked atoms" expound-
ed by Lowes) in the essay by Howard Schless entitled
"Chaucer and Dante." Details of publication can be found
below, pp. 18-19, under the name of the editor of the collection, Dorothy Bethurum.

[30]The Discarded Image: An Introduction to Medieval and
Renaissance Literature (Cambridge, Eng.: Cambridge
University Press, 1964), p. 193. The context of the quotation from Lewis is as follows: "Nearly all of us, when we
first began reading medieval poetry, got the impression that
the poets were unable to keep to the point. We may even
have thought that they were drifting with the stream of
consciousness. The revived study of medieval Rhetoric--a
welcome novelty in twentieth-century medievalism--puts an

which has had a profound impact on Chaucer studies, took
its initial force and much of its subsequent direction from
the publication (in 1924) of Edmund Faral's edition of the
major Latin rhetorical manuals of the late twelfth and early
thirteenth centuries, and from the publication (in 1926) of
J. M. Manly's discussion of the influence of this body of
rhetorical teaching on Chaucer's poetry.[31] The flood of
articles on the general subject of "Chaucer and the Rhetoricians" which has appeared since 1926 would suggest that
acceptance of the influence of formal rhetoric on Chaucer's
poetry has itself become something of a rhetorical "common-
place" in modern criticism.[32] James J. Murphy has count-
ed "more than forty" studies, not counting dissertations,
which have appeared since 1926, all of which are "devoted
to the thesis that Chaucer, in composing many of his poetical works, consciously followed the precepts of what Manly
termed 'rhetoricians.'"[33]

---

end to that idea. For good or ill the digressiveness of the
medieval writers is the product not of nature but of art."
   [31]Edmund Faral, Les Arts Poètiques du XIIe et du XIIIe
Siècle (Paris, 1924); see Griffith, p. 119. Manly's essay is
cited in note 2 of this Introduction.
   [32]Cf. J. A. W. Bennett, The Parlement of Foules, p. 25
(see below, p. 93): "If modern Chaucer criticism has es-
tablished one thing more firmly than another, it is the poet's
knowledge and mastery of the rhetorical modes as promul-
gated by half a dozen earlier writers, French and English,
and as practiced by the poets in whom he was deeply read
and by whom he was greatly influenced."
   [33]"A New Look at Chaucer and the Rhetoricians," RES,
15, 1964, 1-20. In a series of important articles Murphy
has questioned the existence in fourteenth-century England
of what he writes might fairly be described as a "Cult of
Vinsauf": "Indeed, the ubiquity of grammatical texts and the
paucity of rhetorical texts is so marked in fourteenth-century
English records that on this ground alone there might be
some reason for supposing that Chaucer and his contempo-
raries may have participated in a 'grammatical' rather than

It is obviously beyond the scope of an Introduction of this size and nature even to attempt to summarize the fruits of so much scholarly investigation. I should, however, like to point out that this "welcome novelty" has throughout most of its life been beset by two closely related problems: (1) How is it possible to write the history of rhetoric in the Middle Ages without at the same time prejudging it as a debasement of classical forms; and (2) how is it possible to make this body of rhetorical theory, once described, applicable to criticism--particularly to stylistic and structural analysis-- of Chaucer's poetry. Richard McKeon, addressing himself to the first problem in 1942, comments that "scholarly labors have reconstructed only a brief and equivocal history for rhetoric during the Middle Ages, " and in a note documenting these labors, McKeon writes that "the history of rhetoric has more recently been extended to the Middle Ages, but it is always rhetoric in some particular sense, applied to some particular subject, and the history is usually negative or at least deprecatory. "[34] The comprehensive and sympathetic treatment of medieval rhetoric which McKeon noted as lacking in 1942 was handsomely supplied in 1948 with the publication of Ernst Robert Curtius' Europäische Literatur und lateinisches Mittelalter. [35] Since its publication, this book has become a veritable mine of information and suggestion for the student of medieval literature. [36]

The second problem, the practical problem of turning rhetorical theory to critical use, is the subject of Robert O. Payne's The Key of Remembrance, the last critical work

---

a 'rhetorical' tradition" ("A New Look, " p. 4). Articles by Murphy published before 1964 are listed below, pp. 45-46.

[34]"Rhetoric in the Middle Ages, " Speculum, 17, 1942, 1-32 (see Griffith, p. 123); the first quotation appears on page 1; the second is contained in note 1 on p. 2.

[35](Bern: A. Francke Verlag); see below, p. 43, for notice of Willard R. Trask's translation of this book.

[36]See, for example, the Introduction (especially pp. xvi-xvii) to James J. Wilhelm, The Cruelest Month (see note 2 above).

which I shall consider in this Introduction. [37] Payne's study
is important in the history of modern criticism of Chaucer,
not because it provides a definitive solution to the problem,
but rather because it re-examines that problem from a perspective which is radically different from, for example,
Manly's. This new perspective is the product of a set of
assumptions about the nature of poetry as verbal artifice
and about the range of attitudes which a poet, medieval or
modern, may reasonably be expected to take toward the
traditional materials and techniques of his craft. When
Chaucer is viewed from this perspective, he is seen as
neither a slave of nor a rebel to the rhetorical tradition; he
is a conscious manipulator of it. His self-awareness is the
true subject of a number of his poems, most notably the
Prologue to the Legend of Good Women, and verbal artifice
is the principal means by which traditional values are pre-
served in time: "In summary, Chaucer started from (and
never grew away from) the primary definitions of purpose
and method in art as laid down by the orthodox tradition in
medieval aesthetics: poetry is a process of manipulating
language so that the wisdom evolved in the past will become
available, applicable, and operative in the present" (p. 89).
    The Key of Remembrance is not an easy book to follow or
to describe. The difficulty for the reader results in part
from the scope of the book and in part from Payne's order-
ing and presentation of his subject. The general plan of the
book is, however, clearly laid down for the reader on page 8:
"My over-all scheme is first to characterize the rhetorical
poetic which seems to have provided Chaucer's fundamental
assumptions about the nature of poetry, then to assemble the
direct evidence for his concern with the theoretical questions, and finally to indicate how his poems themselves
reflect a range of experiments toward answering the questions."
    The "rhetorical poetic" which Payne characterizes in
Chapter i is not a "debasement" of classical forms but
rather, following Curtius, an "example of a medieval

------

[37]For details of publication, see below, p. 25.

reconstruction out of classical ruins" (p. 22). What could
not be salvaged from the ruins of classical rhetoric and
turned to the use of Christian idealism was a fully developed
theory of Inventio as defined, for example, by the anony-
mous author of the Rhetorica ad Herennium: "Invention is
the devising of matter, true or plausible, that would make
the case convincing. "[38] All useful knowledge had already
been "invented" and revealed to man both directly in Scrip-
ture and indirectly through the operation of the Divine Will
in the creation and history of the universe. Preservation
and communication of this knowledge thus take the place of
invention within the "rhetorical poetic" of the Middle Ages:
"Tradition itself--both as meaningful historical pattern or
accurate literary constructs by previous observers, and as
workable analyses of means--becomes a pattern for imita-
tion and a substitute for ancient 'invention'" (p. 46). Thus
the authors of the artes poeticae, those practical manuals
in which rhetorical theory is applied to the composition of
(Latin) poetry, devoted by far the greater part of their
treatises to consideration of amplification and stylistic
elaboration of traditional matter rather than to a discussion
of inventio--the "devising of matter. " Payne has succeeded
in this chapter in reassessing the artes poeticae by demon-
strating that they are a significant manifestation of a "rhetorical poetic" which is itself coherent and purposeful. The
authors of these treatises were not the inventors of the
theory of poetry which is expressed in them.
     Payne turns (in Chapter ii) to an examination of those
passages in which Chaucer voices continuing concern
throughout his career with practical solutions to aesthetic
problems similar to those formulated in the artes poeticae.
The recurring theme of these passages is the difficulty of
arriving at the stylistic and formal means by which the wisdom of the past, the authority of "olde books, " may be

------

[38]Translated by Harry Caplan in the Loeb Classical Library (London: Heinemann, 1954); cf. Payne's statement
(on p. 44): "Inventio had been for Aristotle and Cicero alike,
a genuine process of discovery through rational activity. "

related in meaningful ways to the experience of the present.
The stylistic means by which Chaucer bridged past and
present were themselves a part of the "rhetorical poetic"
and were available to him from a variety of sources: the
codifications of amplificatory devices to be found in the
manuals and in the example of vernacular poetry, both
French and Italian, which is roughly contemporaneous to
those rhetorical manuals. [39] One of the many virtues of
Payne's study is that Chaucer's relationship to the artes is
consistently seen as one of congruence rather than one of
direct influence: "And we may well even find poets in the
vernacular absorbing these same standards of composition
from two or three different sources: quite indirectly,
through their predecessors in the vernaculars; at second
hand, through Latin poetry; or directly from the sources
themselves. Such is demonstrably the case with Dante and
Chaucer, who, despite their differences in poetic personality, have a common consciousness of their own art and of
the traditional bases upon which it rests" (p. 53).

The formal means by which Chaucer attempted to solve
the problems imposed by "a poetics of tradition" result in
a series of experiments with structure which are "indicative
of three different tentative solutions in Chaucer's poetry to
the aesthetic problems which I have been discussing"
(p. 116). These various solutions, which show Chaucer at
his most inventive, are treated--with varying degrees of
success--in the remaining chapters of the book.

The Key of Remembrance is, finally, a determined examination of Chaucer's poetic which begins with a re-evaluation of the "rhetorical poetic" of the Middle Ages and
returns to detailed analyses of the stylistic and structural
means by which Chaucer was able to accommodate the wisdom of the past to the experience of the present in a form
that would be able to withstand the erosion of the future.

_____

[39]Cf. Muscatine, p. 6 ("In this case the same medieval
tradition of rhetoric, based on Latin models, is behind the
French, the Italian, and the English poetry"), and Muscatine's reference to Curtius, pp. 383-85.

How well he succeeded can be measured only by the pressure which his poetry exerts to be rightly understood by each
generation of readers. Payne's study of Chaucer's poetic is
one response to that pressure. The book is noteworthy for
the attitudes its author has taken toward the complex relationship of the poet to the tradition within which he worked,
as well as for Payne's reading of those poems in which
Chaucer confronts that relationship directly. The book
marks how far we have come in defining a poetic large
enough to account for Chaucer's most mature achievement;
it is also a book that suggests how far we have yet to go.

I am well aware that this essay is neither a "balanced"
nor a comprehensive introduction to all the criticism of
Chaucer that has been written in the last decade or so. I
have not, for example, considered in detail the writing of
those who would explicate all medieval poetry in light of the
techniques of scriptural exegesis. My reason for not doing
so is simply this: proponents of this approach, most notably
D. W. Robertson, Jr., have advanced in the last fifteen
years an immensely learned case in support of the historical necessity for interpreting allegorically all medieval
poetry, including Chaucer's. This impressive prolegome-
non to criticism has not, as yet, produced a commensurate
body of Chaucer criticism which would justify the theoretical underpinnings. I have, therefore, limited myself to what
I trust is an accurate summary of that body of theory. An
Introduction such as this one, written ten years hence, will
no doubt have to take into account a large and significant
body of Chaucer criticism based upon the theory and techniques of medieval exegesis.
I am also aware that in this essay I have omitted from discussion a number of works that would have been a pleasure
to consider: D. S. Brewer's splendid edition of The Parlement of Foulys, Wolfgang Clemen's Chaucer's Early Poetry,
J. A. W. Bennett's The Parlement of Foules, and Sanford B.
Meech's Design in Chaucer's Troilus. Each of these books
has added significantly to our critical understanding of Chaucer's accomplishment. Limitations of space have also pre-
vented me from discussing other important contributions by

a number of distinguished Chaucerians. Articles by Robert A. Pratt (see below, pp. 33-34), Morton Bloomfield
(p. 96), and Ralph Baldwin (p. 52) would certainly receive
detailed attention in a more extended essay. This Introduction is, necessarily, selective, evaluative, and tentative. I
have chosen for extensive discussion those critical works
that have, in my judgment, contributed most substantially to
an emerging criticism of Chaucer which is distinctively
modern.

ABBREVIATIONS

A and A	Anelida and Arcite
AB	Anglia Beiblatt
AES	Abstracts of English Studies
AHR	American Historical Review
Ang	Anglia
AnM	Annuale Mediaevale (Duquesne University)
ANQ	American Notes and Queries (New Haven, Connecticut; Vol. I, 1962--)
AQ	Arizona Quarterly
Archiv	Archiv für das Studium der neueren Sprachen und Literaturen
BA	Books Abroad
BB	Bulletin of Bibliography
BC	Book Collector
BD	Book of the Duchess
BJRL	Bulletin of the John Rylands Library
BMQ	British Museum Quarterly
BUSE	Boston University Studies in English
CBEL	Cambridge Bibliography of English Literature (including Vol. V: Supplement)
CE	College English
CEA	College English Association Critic
CJ	Classical Journal
CL	Comparative Literature

CLAJ	College Language Association Journal (Morgan State College, Baltimore, Maryland)
ClT	Clerk's Tale
CookT	Cook's Tale
CQ	Critical Quarterly (London)
CRAS	The Centennial Review of Arts and Science (Michigan State University)
Crit	Criticism
CT	The Canterbury Tales
CW	The Catholic World
CYT	Canon's Yeoman's Tale
DA	Dissertation Abstracts
DUJ	Durham University Journal
EA	Études Anglaises
EC	Essays in Criticism
EHR	English Historical Review
EJ	English Journal
ELH	English Literary History
EM	English Miscellany
Eng	English, Magazine of the English Association (London)
ES	Englische Studien
E Stud	English Studies
Expl	Explicator
FrankT	Franklin's Tale
FriarT	Friar's Tale
GP	General Prologue
Hist	History
HF	House of Fame
HLQ	Huntington Library Quarterly
HSELL	Hiroshima Studies in English Language and Literature
JA	Journal of Aesthetics and Art Criticism
JAF	Journal of American Folklore
JEGP	Journal of English and Germanic Philology
JHI	Journal of the History of Ideas
KN	Kwartalnik Neofilologiczny (Warsaw)
KnT	Knight's Tale
Leeds	Proceedings of the Leeds Philosophical and Literary Society (Literary and Historical Section)

LGW	Legend of Good Women
List	The Listener
LJ	Library Journal
MAE	Medium Aevum
M and H	Medievalia et Humanistica (Boulder, Colorado)
ManT	Manciple's Tale
Med Stud	Mediaeval Studies (Toronto)
Mel	Melibeus
MerT	Merchant's Tale
MilT	Miller's Tale
MissQ	Mississippi Quarterly
MLN	Modern Language Notes
MLQ	Modern Language Quarterly
MLR	Modern Language Review
MLT	Man of Law's Tale
MonT	Monk's Tale
MP	Modern Philology
MS	Moderna Spraak (Stockholm)
Neophil	Neophilologus
NM	Neuphilologische Mitteilungen
NMQ	New Mexico Quarterly
NPT	Nun's Priest's Tale
NQ	Notes and Queries (New Series; Vol. I, 1954--)
NS	Die Neuren Sprachen
NYHTB	New York Herald Tribune Book Review
NYTB	New York Times Book Review
Obs	Observer
OL	Orbis Litterarum
PardT	Pardoner's Tale
ParsT	Parson's Tale
PBSA	Papers of the Bibliographical Society of America
PF	Parliament of Fowls
PhyT	Physician's Tale
PMASAL	Publications of the Michigan Academy of Sciences, Arts, and Letters (Ann Arbor, Michigan)
PMLA	Publications of the Modern Language Association of America
PQ	Philological Quarterly
PriorT	Prioress' Tale

Prol	Prologue
QJS	Quarterly Journal of Speech
QQ	Queen's Quarterly
QR	Quarterly Review
Reeve'sT	Reeve's Tale
REL	Review of English Literature (Leeds)
RES	Review of English Studies
Rom	Romania
RR	Romanic Review
SAQ	South Atlantic Quarterly
Script	Scriptorium
Shen	Shenandoah
ShT	Shipman's Tale
SMS	Studier i Modern Sprakvetenskap (Stockholm)
SN	Studia Neophilologica
SNT	Second Nun's Tale
SP	Studies in Philology
Spec	Speculum
Spect	Spectator
SQ	Shakespeare Quarterly
SqT	Squire's Tale
SumT	Summoner's Tale
T and C	Troilus and Criseyde
TLS	Times Literary Supplement (London)
TSE	Tulane Studies in English
TSL	Tennessee Studies in Literature
TSLL	Texas Studies in Literature and Language
UCSLL	University of Colorado Studies in Language and Literature
UMSE	University of Mississippi Studies in English
UTQ	University of Toronto Quarterly
WBPro	Wife of Bath's Prologue
WBT	Wife of Bath's Tale
WVUB	West Virginia University Bulletin (Philological Papers)
YCGL	Yearbook of Comparative and General Literature (University of North Carolina Studies in Comparative Literature)
YWES	Year's Work in English Studies (Chaucer Section)
ZAA	Zeitschrift für Anglistik und Amerikanistik

Bibliography of Chaucer, 1954-63

BIBLIOGRAPHY

See Griffith, pp. 5-12.

THE CAMBRIDGE BIBLIOGRAPHY OF ENGLISH LITERA-
TURE. Vol. V (Supplement), edited by George Watson.
General Editor, F. W. Bateson. Cambridge Univ Press,
1957.
  This supplement continues the listings of the CBEL
from 1930 to "the beginning of the year 1955." The Chaucer Section (pp. 130-45) was prepared by D. S. Brewer
and revised by Dr. J. A. W. Bennett.
  Rev: Claude E. Jones, BB, 22, 1958, 104-5; L. W.
Hanson, Library, 13, 1958, 208-10; John Hayward, BC,
7, 1958, 82 and 85; George L. McKay, PBSA, 52, 1958,
68-70; Gwin J. Kolb, MP, 56, 1958-59, 197-203; Herbert
Cahoon, LJ, 83, 1958, 61; G. T. Senn, Archiv, 196,
1960, 92-93; R. Juchhoff, Ang, 79, 1961-62, 214-16.
CHAUCER RESEARCH, 1954-1963. Reports No. 15-24 of
the Committee on Research and Bibliography of the Chaucer Group of the Modern Language Association of America. Edited by Thomas A. Kirby (Ch.), Martin M. Crow,
George R. Coffman (1954-55), Dudley D. Griffith (1956-
60), and Charles Muscatine (1962--).
  This extremely valuable research tool is available in
mimeographed form at the annual meeting of the Modern
Language Association of America (Group 3). "Copies of

the present report ($. 25) may be obtained from the chair-
man of the committee, whose address is Department of
English, Louisiana State University, Baton Rouge 3,
Louisiana. "

THE ENGLISH ASSOCIATION. The Year's Work in English
Studies, 1921--. Edited by Beatrice White and T. S.
Dorsch. Oxford Univ Press.

 YWES contains descriptive notices of selected articles
and books. Beginning with Vol. XXXIV (1955 for 1953), the
author of the Chaucer Section has been Miss Joyce Bazire.
 Rev: Vol₀ XXXVI (1957 for 1955), G. S. Ivy, DUJ, 20,
1959, 142-43; W. Fischer, Ang, 77, 1959, 75-76; Vol.
XXXVII (1958 for 1956), G. S. Ivy, DUJ, 20, 1959, 142-
43; W. Fischer, Ang, 77, 1959, 208; C. J₀ Sisson, MLR,
54, 1959, 451; Vol. XXXVIII (1959 for 1957), E. G. Stanley, NQ, 7, 1960, 353-54; Horst Oppel, NS, 1960, 365-
66; R. W. Zandvoort, E Stud, 42, 1961, 395-96; R. W.
Dent, SQ, 12, 1961, 145-46; Henry Pettit, MLR, 56,
1961, 399-400; Vol. XXXIX (1960 for 1958), R. W. Zandvoort, E Stud, 42, 1961, 395-96; Henry Pettit, MLR, 56,
1961, 399-400.

GRIFFITH, DUDLEY D₀, Ed. Bibliography of Chaucer,
1909-1953. Seattle (Univ of Washington Publications in
Language and Literature, Vol. XIII), 1955.
 Rev: William White, BB, 21, 1955, 152; TLS, Sept 2,
1955, 514; Joseph G. Fucilla, JEGP, 55, 1956, 501-2;
Hermann M. Flasdieck, Ang, 74, 1956, 252-53; Rolf
Berndt, ZAA, 4, 1956, 494-96; F. Mossé, EA, 9, 1956,
42; Howard R. Patch, MLN, 72, 1957, 210-12; J. A. W.
Bennett, RES, 8, 1957, 180-81; Ursula Brown, MAE, 27,
1958, 39-43.

INTERNATIONAL GUIDE TO MEDIEVAL STUDIES: A Quarterly Index to Periodical Literature. Darien, Conn.: American Bibliographic Service. Vol. I (No. 1), June, 1961--.

LINGUISTIC BIBLIOGRAPHY. Vol. IX for the Year 1954
(1956), Vol. X for 1955 (1957); for 1956 (1958), etc. Published by the Permanent International Committee of Linguistics with a Grant from the United Nations Educational,
Scientific, and Cultural Organization. Utrecht-Brussels:
Spectrum.

THE MEDIAEVAL ACADEMY OF AMERICA. Bibliography
of American Periodical Literature, 1934--.
This bibliography is published quarterly in Speculum: A
Journal of Mediaeval Studies; the list of "Books Received"
(quarterly) should also be noted.
THE MODERN HUMANITIES RESEARCH ASSOCIATION.
Annual Bibliography of English Language and Literature,
1920--. Edited by various hands; beginning with Vol.
XXXIII (1962 for 1957-58) by Marjory Rigby, Charles
Nilon, and others.
The publication of the MHRA bibliography was delayed
by the war; as Griffith notes (p. 9), Vol. XXIV (for 1943-
44) was "ready for the press" in 1955 and was published in
1956. A register of volume numbers and publication dates
follows: XXIV (1956 for 1943-44); XXV (1956 for 1945);
XXVI (1958 for 1946); XXVII (1956 for 1947); XXVIII (1957
for 1948); XXIX (1957 for 1949); XXX (1958 for 1950-52);
XXXI (1960 for 1953-54); XXXII (1961 for 1955-56); XXXIII
(1962 for 1957-58); XXXIV (1962 for 1959); XXXV (1963
for 1960); XXXVI (1964 for 1961).
MODERN LANGUAGE ASSOCIATION OF AMERICA. American Bibliography, 1922-1956. International Bibliography,
1957--. Edited (beginning with Vol. LXVII issued in 1952)
by Paul A. Brown, and others.
This bibliography is published annually as the second
number of each volume of PMLA; each volume contains
the bibliography for the preceding year.
NATIONAL COUNCIL OF TEACHERS OF ENGLISH. Abstracts of English Studies, 1958--. Edited by John B.
Shipley, and others. Boulder, Colo.
Issued ten times a year (Vols. I-IV contain twelve is-
sues). The abstracts (averaging less than 100 words) often
appear within three months of the publication of the article
abstracted. Each issue is indexed, and an index to each
volume is published annually.
---------- (The Committee on Literary Scholarship and the
Teaching of English). Contemporary Literary Scholarship:
A Critical Review. Edited by Lewis Leary. New York:
Appleton-Century-Crofts, 1958. See "Beowulf, Chaucer,
and Their Backgrounds," by George K. Anderson, pp. 25-52.

Professor Anderson discusses (on p. 25 and pp. 30-52)
the Chaucer scholarship written between 1930 and 1957.
Rev: Don Geiger, QJS, 44, 1958, 447-48; Seven. Cent.
News, 16, 1958, 45-46; Haskell M. Block, CL, 11, 1959,
270-75; TLS, July 17, 1959, 424.

PROGRESS OF MEDIEVAL AND RENAISSANCE STUDIES IN
THE UNITED STATES AND CANADA. Edited by S. Harrison Thomson. Bulletins Nos. 22-25 (1953-60) published
at the Univ of Colorado, Boulder, Colo.

In the "Foreword" to Bulletin No. 25, Professor Thomson remarks that "the future of the Progress is . . . un-
certain."

QUARTERLY CHECK-LIST OF MEDIEVALIA: An International Index of Current Books, Monographs, Brochures
and Separates, Darien, Conn.: American Bibliographic
Service. Vol. I (No. 1), Jan, 1958--.

ZESMER, DAVID M. Guide to English Literature: From
Beowulf through Chaucer and Medieval Drama. With Bibliographies by Stanley B. Greenfield. New York: Barnes
and Noble (College Outline Series, 53), 1961.

The items in the Chaucer bibliography (pp. 353-74) have
been selected and annotated with "the general reader, the
college undergraduate, and the graduate student" in mind
as an audience.

Rev: Robert P. Creed, CE, 23, 1961-62, 162.

LIFE

See Griffith, pp. 13-27.

BLAND, D. S. When Was Chaucer Born? TLS, April 26, 1957, 264.

Mr. Bland's suggestion that Chaucer was born in 1345-46 elicited the following responses in the letter columns of TLS: Margaret Galway, May 10, 289 and July 12, 427; C. E. Welch, May 17, 305; G. C. G. Hall, June 28, 397.

BREWER, DEREK. Chaucer in His Time. London: T. Nelson, 1963.

CHUTE, MARCHETTE. Geoffrey Chaucer of England. New York: E. P. Dutton, 1958. Paperback reprint (Everyman). London: Four Square Books, 1962 (rev. ed.).

For review, see Griffith, p. 16.

FISHER, JOHN H. A Calendar of Documents Relating to the Life of John Gower the Poet. JEGP, 58, 1959, 1-23.

See esp. Sect. 12 (pp. 21-22): "Chaucer gives Gower his power of attorney."

GALWAY, MARGARET. "Pullesdon" in the Life-Records of Chaucer. NQ, 4, 1957, 371-74.

----------. Chaucer's Journeys in 1368. TLS, April 4, 1958, 183.

----------. Court Poets' I. O. U. 's. TLS, Oct 16, 1953, 668.

7

----------. Walter Roet and Philippa Chaucer. NQ, 1,
  1954, 48-49.
----------. Philippa Pan·, Philippa Chaucer. MLR, 55,
  1960, 481-87.
HONORÉ-DUVERGÉ, SUZANNE. Chaucer en Espagne (1366).
  Vol. II, pp. 9-13 of Recueil de Travaux offert à M. Clovis
  Brunel par ses Amis, Collègues et Élèves. Paris: Mém-
  oires et Documents Publiés par la Société de l'École des
  Chartres, 12, 1955. 2 vols.
LONDON, H. STANFORD. Gerard Legh, Herald. NQ, 2,
  1955, 271-72.
    See earlier article by Schoeck, below in this section.
LOUNSBURY, T. R. Studies in Chaucer: His Life and Writings. 3 vols. Reprinted. New York: Russell and Russell,
  1962.
NEVILLE, MARIE. Chaucer and St. Clare. JEGP, 55, 1956,
  423-30.
    The Eagle's oath "by Seynte Clare" (HF, 1066) may have
  had particular significance for Chaucer the poet.
SCHOECK, R. J. Gerard Legh, Herald. NQ, 2, 1955, 140.
    See also H. Stanford London, above in this section.
WILLIAMS, GEORGE. Chaucer's Long Lease and the Date
  of His Birth. NQ, 7, 1960, 168.
    Rejects Stevenson's conjecture (MLN, 50, 1935, 318-
  22) that Chaucer's age in 1399 can be determined by the
  amount of rent he paid annually for his last house.

MANUSCRIPTS

See Griffith, pp. 28-40.

BAKER, DONALD C. The Bradshaw Order of the Canterbury
Tales: A Dissent. NM, 63, 1962, 245-61.
CAMPBELL, JACKSON J. A New Troilus Fragment. PMLA,
73, 1958, 305-8.
Text, plates and discussion of the Cecil Fragment; see
YWES review (Vol. XXXIX for 1958) for list of "undoubted
misreadings" in "Campbell's diplomatic transcription. "
DEARING, VINTON ADAMS. A Manual of Textual Analysis.
Berkeley: Univ of California Press, 1959.
Examples drawn from ten MSS and two early prints of
Chaucer's Complaint to His Purse.
D(OYLE), A. I. Unrecorded Chaucerian Manuscript.
Durham Philobiblon, 1, 1953, 54-55.
FRANCIS, W. NELSON. Graphemic Analysis of Late Middle
English Manuscripts. Spec, 37, 1962, 32-47.
FURNIVALL, F. J. , Ed. The Booke of the Duchesse, Made
by Geffrey Chawcyer at the Request of the Duke of Lancas-
tar, Pitiously Complaynynge the Deathe of the Sayd Duch-
esse Blanche. Lexington, Ky.: Anvil Press, 1954.
"The text of this edition is the one of the Chaucer Soci-
ety, First Series, XXIV, edited by F. J. Furnivall, 1871,
from the Fairfax MS. 16, Bodleian Library. "
HARTUNG, ALBERT EDWARD. A Study of the Textual

Affiliations of Chaucer's Melibeus Considered in Its Relation to the French Source. DA, 17, 2259-60. Lehigh Univ,
1957.

McINTOSH, ANGUS. The Analysis of Written Middle English.
Trans. of the Philological Society, 1956, 26-55.

OWEN, CHARLES A., JR. The Canterbury Tales: Early
Manuscripts and Relative Popularity. JEGP, 54, 1955,
104-10.

ROBBINS, ROSSELL HOPE. A Love Epistle by "Chaucer."
MLR, 49, 1954, 289-92.
  The poem in question is wrongly ascribed to Chaucer in
Trinity College, Cambridge, MS 599 (R. 3. 19).

----------. The Findern Anthology. PMLA, 69, 1954, 610-
42.

SEVERS, J. BURKE. Did Chaucer Rearrange the Clerk's
Envoy? MLN, 69, 1954, 472-78.

----------. Author's Revision in Block C of the Canterbury
Tales. Spec, 29, 1954, 512-30.

EDITIONS WITH NOTES

See Griffith, pp. 41-48.

BARBER, MARJORIE M. Selections from Chaucer's Canterbury Tales. London: Macmillan; New York: St. Martin's Press, 1961.
A volume in the Scholar's Library Series.
BAUGH, ALBERT C. Chaucer's Major Poetry. New York: Appleton-Century-Crofts, 1963.
BENNETT, J. A. W. The Knight's Tale. London: Harrap, 1954; 2nd rev. ed. Harrap, 1958.
Rev: D. L. Sims, MAE, 24, 1955, 128-29; H. S. Bennett, RES, 6, 1955, 331.
BETHURUM, DOROTHY, and RANDALL STEWART. Chaucer and Shakespeare: The Dramatic Vision. New York: Scott, Foresman and Co., 1954.
Vol. IV of a textbook called Living Masterpieces of English Literature; text follows Skeat.
BREWER, D. S. The Parlement of Foulys. London and Edinburgh: Thomas Nelson and Sons; New York: Barnes and Noble, 1960. (Nelson's Medieval and Renaissance Library.)
Rev: J. A. Burrow, RES, 12, 1961, 413-15; Dorothy Bethurum, MAE, 30, 1961, 195-98; Peter Dronke, NQ, 8, 1961, 475-76; Charles Muscatine, MLR, 57, 1962, 81-82.

BURNS, SISTER MARY FLORENCE, C. S. J. A Textual
Study of Thomas Tyrwhitt's Edition of the Canterbury
Tales (1775-1778). DA, 22, 1154. Columbia Univ, 1961.
From the abstract: "The final conclusion to be drawn
from this study, then, is that Tyrwhitt's edition of 1775
constituted the first modern critical edition of the Canter-
bury Tales."
CAWLEY, A. C. The Canterbury Tales. London: Dent;
New York: Dutton, 1958. (Everyman's Library, 307.)
The text has been newly re-edited for this series from
the Ellesmere MS; for listing of older editions in this ser-
ies (edited by Burrell), see Griffith, p. 42.
Rev: Ursula Brown, RES, 11, 1960, 312-14; R. W.
Zandvoort, E Stud, 43, 1962, 110-15.
CHAUCER, GEOFFREY. Fünf Canterbury-Geschichten.
Five Canterbury Tales. Ebenhausen bei München: Edition
Langewiesche-Brandt, 1958.
COGHILL, NEVILL, and C. TOLKIEN. The Pardoner's
Tale. London: Harrap, 1958.
Rev: R. W. Zandvoort, E Stud, 43, 1962, 110-15.
----------, and J. R. R. TOLKIEN. The Nun's Priest's
Tale. London: Harrap, 1959.
Rev: R. W. Zandvoort, E Stud, 43, 1962, 110-15.
COOK, DANIEL. The Canterbury Tales of Geoffrey Chau-
cer. A Selection Edited with Introduction and Notes. Gar-
den City, N.Y.: Doubleday, 1961. (Anchor Books, 265.)
General Prologue and five tales (including prologues and
links); text and glosses on facing pages.
DONALDSON, E. T. Chaucer's Poetry: An Anthology for
the Modern Reader. New York: Ronald Press, 1958.
Rev: J. B. Bessinger. Chaucer: A Parliament of Cri-
tics, UTQ, 29, 1959, 91-96.
ELLIOTT, R. W. V. Chaucer's Prologue to the Canterbury
Tales. Oxford: Blackwell, 1960 (Notes on English Litera-
ture); New York: Barnes and Noble, 1963.
FRASER, RUSSELL A. The Court of Venus. Durham, N.C.:
Duke Univ Press, 1955; Cambridge Univ Press, 1956.
Rev: R. H. Griffith, Spec, 31, 1956, 508-9; Kenneth
Muir, MLR, 52, 1957, 248-49; Jean Robertson, RES, 8,
1957, 282-83.

HODGSON, PHYLLIS. The Franklin's Tale. London: Athlone Press (Univ of London); New York: Oxford Univ Press, 1960.
> Rev: R. T. Davies, NQ, 7, 1960, 478-79; A. R. Tellier, EA, 14, 1961, 140; R. W. Zandvoort, E Stud, 43, 1962, 110-15.

PRICE, DEREK J. The Equatorie of the Planetis. With a Linguistic Analysis by R. M. Wilson. Cambridge Univ Press, 1955.
> Rev: Curt A. Zimansky, MLN, 71, 1956, 70-76; Robert W. Ackerman, PQ, 35, 1956, 220-23; Roland M. Smith, JEGP, 57, 1958, 533-37 (review article); H. G. Wright, MAE, 28, 1959, 68-69.

ROBINSON, F. N. The Works of Geoffrey Chaucer. 2nd ed. Boston: Houghton Mifflin; London: Oxford Univ Press, 1957.
> Rev: Vernon P. Helming, Spec, 33, 1958, 123-25; TLS, June 13, 1958, 327; Arthur Sale, Cambridge Rev, 79, 233, 235; Tauno F. Mustanoja, NM, 59, 1958, 62-63; Barnett Kottler, CE, 20, 1959, 53-54; D. S. Brewer, MLR, 54, 1959, 251-52; P. Mroczkowski, KN, No. 1, 1959, 64-67; R. W. Zandvoort, E Stud, 43, 1962, 110-15.

ROBINSON, F. W. The Knight's Tale. London: Brodie, 1960.

SPEHAR, ELIZABETH MARIE. Chaucer's Anelida and Arcite: A New Edition. DA, 23, 1010. Univ of Colorado, 1962.

WALLIS, N. HARDY. Canterbury Colloquies: A New Arrangement of the Prologue and End-Links of the Canterbury Tales to Show Their Dramatic Significance. London: Brodie, 1957.

WINTERICH, JOHN T. The Works of Geoffrey Chaucer: A Facsimile of the William Morris Kelmscott Chaucer. Cleveland: World Publishing Company, 1958.
> Reproduces the Edward Burne-Jones illustrations; introduction and glossary supplied by John T. Winterich.
> Rev: NYHTB, Feb 22, 1958, 11.

WRIGHT, H. G. Thomas Speght as a Lexicographer and Annotator of Chaucer's Works. E Stud, 40, 1959, 194-208.

ZANCO, AURELIO. Chaucer Minore. (Collana di lettera-
ture moderne, 9.) Naples: Edizioni Scientifiche Italiane,
1959.
     Rev: Howard R. Patch, JEGP, 59, 1960, 728-30.

MODERNIZATIONS AND TRANSLATIONS

See Griffith, pp. 49-57.

BARNOUW, ADRIAAN J. Troilus en Criseyde. Haarlem:
H. D. Tjeenk Willink and Zoon, 1955.
  Rev: R. W. Zandvoort, E Stud, 37, 1956, 192-93.
CHATFIELD, MINOTTE McINTOSH. Chaucer Translation
in the Romantic Era. DA, 22, 3641. Lehigh Univ, 1961.
CHAUCER, GEOFFREY. Fünf Canterbury-Geschichten.
Five Canterbury Tales. Ebenhausen bei München: Edition
Langewiesche-Brandt, 1958.
COGHILL, NEVILL. The Canterbury Tales. 2 vols. with
woodcuts by Edna Whyte. London: Folio Society, 1956;
New York: Duschnes, 1957. (Reprint of the 1952 ed.)
----------. The Canterbury Tales. Rev. eds.; Harmonds-
worth, England: Penguin Books, 1958 and 1963. Frequent
reprintings.
  See Griffith, p. 50, for original ed. and reviews.
DONOHUE, JAMES J. The Canterbury Pilgrims and Three
Canterbury Tales. Dubuque, Iowa: The Loras College
Press, 1958.
  Reissue in a single volume of two earlier editions;
verse translation of GP and three tales: PardT, NPT,
SNT.
----------. The Knight's Tale. Dubuque, Iowa: The Loras
College Press, 1958.

15

----------. The Monk's Tale. Dubuque, Iowa: The Loras
    College Press, 1961.
FARJEON, ELEANOR. Tales from Chaucer. London: Ox-
    ford Univ Press; Boston: C. T. Branford Co., 1959.
    Reissue.
        See Griffith, p. 51.
HITCHINS, H. L. Canterbury Tales: Chaucer for Present-
    Day Readers. Preface by John Betjeman. London: John
    Murray, 1956.
        A reissue, with new Preface, of 2nd ed.; see Griffith,
    p. 52.
HOBDAY, J. The Franklin's Tale. London: Brodie, 1962.
    (Chosen English Texts.)
HOPPER, VINCENT F. Chaucer's Canterbury Tales. Selec-
    ted in Interlinear Translation. 8th printing. Great Neck,
    N.Y.: Barron's Educational Series, 1955.
        See Griffith, p. 52, for contents.
        Rev: Germaine Dempster, MLN, 70, 1955, 364-66.
KRAPP, GEORGE PHILIP. Troilus and Cressida. Numerous
    reprints: New York: Random House, 1956 (Modern Li-
    brary); 1957 (Modern Library Paperbacks); London: May-
    flower, 1961; New York: Knopf, 1961 (Vintage Books, 142).
        See Griffith, p. 53, for earlier printings and reviews.
LEHNERT, M. Ausgewählte Canterbury Erzählungen. Halle:
    VEB Verlag, 1962.
LUMIANSKY, R. M. Geoffrey Chaucer: The Canterbury
    Tales. Rev. trans. New York: Rinehart, 1954.
        Rev. version of the Simon and Schuster ed. of 1948; see
    Griffith, pp. 53-54, for notice and reviews of original ed.
MORRISON, THEODORE. The Portable Chaucer. New York:
    Viking Press, 1956.
        Reissue of ed. of 1949; see Griffith, p. 54.
MUDRICK, MARVIN. Chaucer as Librettist. PQ, 38, 1959,
    21-29.
        Astringent criticism of many of the modernizations
    listed in this section; concludes that "the Augustans were
    the last English poets who had a sufficiently large com-
    mand of technique and decorum, and sufficient trust in the
    versatility of their idiom, to be capable of turning Chau-
    cer into a contemporary."

SINCLAIR, GILES. Chaucer: Translated or Obliterated?
CE, 15, 1953-54, 272-77.
Bibliography at end of article: Chaucer Modernized.
SPECTOR, R. D. Dryden's Translation of Chaucer: A Problem in Neo-Classical Diction. NQ, 3, 1956, 23-26.
TATLOCK, JOHN S. P., and PERCY MacKAYE. The Modern Readers' Chaucer. New York: Macmillan, 1961.
The most recent of a long series of reprints (see Griffith, p. 56), now issued in paper covers.
WRIGHT, HERBERT G. A Seventeenth-Century Modernisation of the First Three Books of Chaucer's Troilus and Criseyde. (The Cooper Monographs, 5.) Bern: Francke, 1960.
Rev: Gösta Langenfelt, SN, 33, 1961, 347-51; Hans Käsmann, Ang, 80, 1961, 333-34.

GENERAL CRITICISM

See Griffith, pp. 58-80.

BATESON, F. W. Work in Progress II: Renaissance Literature. EC, 13, 1963, 117-31.
References to Chaucer.

BAUM, PAULL F. Chaucer: A Critical Appreciation. Durham, N. C.: Duke Univ Press; Cambridge Univ Press, 1958.
Rev: Herbert Feinstein, QJS, 45, 1959, 81-82; Basil Cottle, JEGP, 58, 1959, 676-78; TLS, June 12, 1959, 350; J. B. Bessenger, Chaucer: A Parliament of Critics, UTQ, 29, 1959, 91-96; George Kane, MLR, 55, 1960, 265-66; John Burrow, EC, 10, 1960, 202-7; Howard R. Patch, MLN, 75, 1960, 51-53; M. M. Crow, MP, 58, 1960, 53-55; Dorothy Bethurum, Spec, 35, 1960, 98-101.

----------. Chaucer's Verse. Durham, N.C.: Duke Univ Press; Cambridge Univ Press, 1961.
See esp. Chapter iii (Art Poetical).
Rev: Ewald Standop, Ang, 80, 1963, 448-53.

BERNDT, ROLF. Einführung in das Studium des Mittelenglischen unter Zugrundlegung des Prologs der Canterbury Tales. Halle/Saale: Niemeyer, 1960.
Rev: B. Trnka, Căsopis pro moderní filologii, 43, 109-10.

BETHURUM, DOROTHY, Ed. Critical Approaches to

Medieval Literature: Selected Papers from the English
Institute, 1958-1959. New York: Columbia Univ Press,
1960.
   Contents: Patristic Exegesis in the Criticism of Medie-
val Literature: E. Talbot Donaldson, The Opposition, pp.
1-26; R. E. Kaske, The Defense, pp. 27-60; Charles
Donahue, Summation, pp. 61-82; Francis Lee Utley, Folk-
lore, Myth, and Ritual, pp. 83-109; Richard Hamilton
Green, Classical Fable and English Poetry in the Four-
teenth Century, pp. 110-33; Howard Schless, Chaucer and
Dante, pp. 134-54; Notes, pp. 155-71.
   Rev: D. S. Brewer, MAE, 31, 1962, 46-49.
BREWER, D. S. Love and Marriage in Chaucer's Poetry.
   MLR, 49, 1954, 461-64.
----------. The Ideal of Feminine Beauty in Medieval Lit-
   erature, Especially "Harley Lyrics," Chaucer, and Some
   Elizabethans. MLR, 50, 1955, 257-69.
----------. Chaucer. (Men and Books Series.) 2nd rev. ed.
   London, Toronto, New York: Longmans, Green, 1960.
   See Griffith, p. 369, for notice and contents of the 1st
   ed.; the following reviews of the 1st ed. (1953) should be
   noted: TLS, Nov 27, 1953, 762; James Kinsley, MAE,
   23, 1954, 53-55. Christopher Hollis. Chaucer and the
   World: This and the Next. The Tablet, 202 (Dec 26, 1953),
   623 (rev. art.). See also reply by James Broderick to the
   Hollis review: Chaucer and St. Ignatius. Ibid., 203 (Jan 2,
   1954), 18.
----------. Chaucer in His Time. London: T. Nelson, 1963.
BRONSON, BERTRAND H. In Search of Chaucer. (The Alexander Lectures, 1959.) Toronto: Univ of Toronto Press;
   London: Oxford Univ Press, 1960. Reissue: Univ of Toronto Press, 1963 (paper).
   Rev: Bertram Colgrave, Spec, 36, 1961, 460-63; R. T.
   Davies, NQ, 8,1961, 398-99; Marie P. Hamilton, AQ, 17,
   1961, 366-69; D. S. Brewer, MLR, 57, 1962, 79-80; J.
   Carey, MAE, 31, 1962, 153-54; R. George Thomas, RES,
   13, 1962, 289-90.
CAVALCANTI, LETICIA NIEDERAUER TAVARES. Sovereignty in Law or Obedience in Marriage: An Analysis of
   the Sovereignty-Obedience Theme and Its Relationship to

the Characterization of Women in the Major Works of
Geoffrey Chaucer. DA, 23, 2522-23. Pennsylvania State
Univ, 1962.

CHESTERTON, GILBERT KEITH. Chaucer. New York:
Sheed and Ward, 1956 (reissue); London: Faber and Fa-
ber, 1959 (2nd ed.)
See Griffith, pp. 61-62, for earlier eds. and reviews.

CLEMEN, WOLFGANG. Chaucers frühe Dichtung. Göttingen
and Zürich: Vandenhoeck and Ruprecht, 1963.
Revision of the author's earlier Der junge Chaucer,
1938; see Griffith, p. 62. For English trans., see next
entry.

----------. Chaucer's Early Poetry (trans. by C. A. M.
Sym). London: Shenval Press, Ltd., 1963; New York:
Barnes and Noble, 1964.

COGHILL, NEVILL. Geoffrey Chaucer. (Writers and Their
Work, No. 79.) London: Longmans, Green, for the British
Council and the National Book League, 1956.

CURRY, WALTER CLYDE. Chaucer and the Mediaeval Sci-
ences. Revised and enlarged ed. New York: Barnes and
Noble; London: George Allen and Unwin, 1960. Reprint,
in paper, of rev. ed.: New York: Barnes and Noble, 1962.
See Griffith, p. 63, for contents and reviews of the 1st
ed.
Rev: Lynn Thorndike, Spec, 35, 1960, 445; Thomas Jay
Garbaty, BA, 35, 1961, 285.

DAVID, ALFRED. Chaucer's Narrator and His Vision of
Courtly Love. Unpub. Doct. Diss., Harvard Univ, 1957.

DE SÉLINCOURT, AUBREY. Six Great Poets: Chaucer,
Pope, Wordsworth, Shelley, Tennyson, the Brownings.
London: H. Hamilton, 1956.
Rev: James Reeves, Obs, March 11, 1956, 17.

DUNLEAVY, GARETH W. Natural Law as Chaucer's Ethi-
cal Absolute. Trans Wisconsin Academy of Sciences, Arts,
and Letters, 52, 1963, 117-87.
Special reference to the Canterbury pilgrims.

FARRELL, WILLIAM J. Chaucer's Use of the Catalogue.
TSLL, 5, 1963, 64-78.

FORD, BORIS, Ed. The Age of Chaucer. (Vol. I of A Guide

to English Literature.) London, Baltimore: Penguin
Books, 1954.
   Contents: Part I: John Speirs, A Survey of Medieval
Verse, pp. 17-67 (pp. 17-32 deal with Chaucer); A. I.
Doyle, English Prose in the Middle Ages, pp. 68-82; Part
II: A. I. Doyle, The Social Context of Medieval Litera-
ture, pp. 85-105; Part III: John Speirs, The Pardoneres
Prologue and Tale, pp. 109-117; David Holbrook, The
Nonne Preestes Tale, pp. 118-28; Part IV: An Anthology
of Medieval Poems (excluding Chaucer); Part V: Biblio-
graphy and short biographical notes.
   Rev: List, 53, 1955, 122; R. M. Lumiansky, Spec, 30,
1955, 104-5.
GAYLORD, ALAN THEODORE. Seed of Felicity: A Study of
the Concepts of Nobility and Gentilesse in the Middle Ages
and in the Works of Chaucer. DA, 20, 3741-42. Princeton
Univ, 1959.
GEROULD, GORDON HALL. Chaucerian Essays. Princeton
Univ Press; London: Oxford Univ Press, 1952.
   A Griffith item (p. 65); the following reviews, which ap-
peared too late to be included in Griffith, should be noted:
P. F. Baum, SAQ, 52, 1953, 478-79; Allan Holaday,
JEGP, 52, 1953, 579-80; Howard R. Patch, MLN, 69,
1954, 374-75; James Kinsley, MAE, 23, 1954, 51-53;
D. S. Brewer, RES, 5, 1954, 403-5; William Lawrence,
Spec, 28, 1954, 394-96; Margaret Galway, E Stud, 36,
1955, 166-67.
GIFFIN, MARY. Studies on Chaucer and His Audience. Hull,
Quebec: Les Éditions l'Éclair, 1956.
   Detailed examination of four poems: SNT, PF, MLT,
and The Complaint of Chaucer to his Purse.
   Rev: M.-M. Dubois, EA, 10, 1957, 245-46; E. M.
Clark, BA, 31, 1957, 420; R. T. Davies, MAE, 27, 1958,
131-34; H. S. Bennett, RES, 9, 1958, 183-84; Ruth Cros-
by, Spec, 33, 1958, 89-91; Hazard Adams, JA, 16, 1958,
534-35; J. B. Bessenger, Chaucer: A Parliament of Critics, UTQ, 29, 1959, 91-96; Theodor Wolpers, Ang, 77,
1960, 349-52; R. Vleeskruyer, E Stud, 41, 1960, 106-8;
Rossell H. Robbins, NM, 59, 1958 (review article).
GRAY, BARBARA JO. Thematic Opposition of Fortuna and

Natura in Chaucer's Narratives. DA, 23, 2517. Tulane
Univ, 1962.
HALL, LOUIS BREWER. An Aspect of the Renaissance in
Gavin Douglas' Edeados. Stud in the Renaissance, 6,
1959, 184-92.
   Douglas as Renaissance translator, Chaucer as medie-
   val adaptor.
HARRISON, THOMAS P. They Tell of Birds: Chaucer, Spen-
ser, Milton, Drayton. Austin: Univ of Texas Press, 1956.
   Rev: R. Bedichek, Southwest Review, 42, 1957, 344-45.
JORDAN, ROBERT M. Chaucer and Time: A Study in Medie-
val Literary Form. Univ of California Diss., 1955.
----------. The Limits of Illusion: Faulkner, Fielding, and
Chaucer. Crit, 2, 1960, 278-305.
   Special reference to narrative personae in CT and T and
   C; cf. Jordan's article in section Troilus and Criseyde.
KLEINSTÜCK, JOHANNES WALTER. Chaucers Stellung in
der mittelalterlichen Literatur. Hamburg: Cram, de
Gruyter and Co., 1956.
   Rev: Karl Hammerle, Ang, 75, 1958, 445-47; D. S.
   Brewer, MLR, 53, 1958, 140; Marjory Rigby, RES, 9,
   1958, 342-43; Ewald Standop, Archiv, 194, 1958-59, 234-
   35; Charles Muscatine, MLN, 74, 1959, 735-37; Claes
   Schaar, E Stud, 41, 1960, 286.
LAWLOR, JOHN. Piers Plowman: An Essay in Criticism.
London: Edward Arnold; New York: Barnes and Noble,
1962.
   Numerous references to Chaucer; comparisons of
   Chaucer with Gower and Langland.
LAWRENCE, WILLIAM WITHERLE. Chaucer and the Can-
terbury Tales. New York: Columbia Univ Press; London:
Oxford Univ Press, 1950.
   A Griffith item (p. 69); the following review should be
   added to those noted by Griffith: Millett Henshaw, MLQ,
   15, 1954, 273-74.
LEACH, MacEDWARD, Ed. Studies in Medieval Literature:
In Honor of Professor Albert Croll Baugh. Philadelphia:
Univ of Pennsylvania Press; London: Oxford Univ Press,
1961.
   The first five essays in this volume have Chaucer as

their subject: Roger Sherman Loomis, Was Chaucer a
Free Thinker?, pp. 21-44; Robert A. Pratt, The Devel-
opment of the Wife of Bath, pp. 45-79; James D. Gordon,
Chaucer's Retraction: A Review of Opinion, pp. 81-96;
Hardin Craig, From Gorgias to Troilus, pp. 97-107;
Francis Lee Utley, Scene-division in Chaucer's Troilus
and Criseyde, pp. 109-38.

LEGOUIS, ÉMILE. Geoffrey Chaucer. Trans. and with a
Preface by L. Lailavoix. New York: Russell and Russell,
1960.
    Reprint of the 1913 ed.; see Griffith, p. 21, for re-
views, and p. 69.

LEWIS, C. S. The Allegory of Love: A Study in Medieval
Tradition. New York: Oxford Univ Press, 1958. Paperback reprint (Galaxy editions).
    See Griffith, pp. 70, 302, 335 for original entries and
reviews.

LOOMIS, LAURA HIBBARD. Adventures in the Middle Ages:
A Memorial Collection of Essays and Studies. New York:
Burt Franklin, 1962.
    This collection contains two essays on the Auchinleck
Manuscript (see Griffith, p. 35) and an essay on Chaucer's
"Tregetoures" (see FrankT for description).

LOUNSBURY, T. R. Studies in Chaucer: His Life and Writings. 3 vols., reprinted. New York: Russell and Russell,
1962.

LOWES, J. LIVINGSTON. Geoffrey Chaucer. (Midland
Books, MB8.) Bloomington, Ind.: Indiana Univ Press,
1958.
    Reprint in paper covers of the 1934 ed., published under
the title Geoffry Chaucer and the Development of His Gen-
ius; see Griffith, p. 71, for reviews.

MacKAIL, J. W. The Springs of Helicon: A Study in the Progress of English Poetry from Chaucer to Milton. Lincoln,
Neb.: Univ of Nebraska Press, 1962.
    Reprint in paper covers of the ed. of 1909; see Griffith,
p. 72, for notice.

MAGOUN, FRANCIS P., JR. A Chaucer Gazeteer. Chicago:
Univ of Chicago Press; Uppsala: Almqvist and Wiksell,
1961.

A compilation (made by Ojars Kratins) of the following
articles by Magoun:
Chaucer's Ancient and Biblical World. Med Stud, 15,
1953, 107-36. Noted and briefly described by Griffith,
p. 72.
Chaucer's Great Britain. Med Stud, 16, 1954, 131-51.
Chaucer's Ancient and Biblical World: Addenda. Med
Stud, 16, 1954, 152-56.
Chaucer's Mediaeval World Outside of Great Britain.
Med Stud, 17, 1955, 117-42.
Rev: NMQ, 31, 1961, 266; Johannes Hedberg, MS, 55,
1961, 277-80; R. T. Davies, NQ, 9, 1962, 159-60; Joyce
Bazire, MLR, 57, 1962, 299-300; J. Burrow, RES, 13,
1962, 216-17; Thomas Finkenstaedt, Ang, 79, 1962, 480-
81.
MAHONEY, JOHN F. Chaucerian Tragedy and the Christian
Tradition. AnM, 3, 1962, 81-99.
Discussion of tragedy in T and C and four of the CT:
KnT, MLT, MonT, and NPT.
MALONE, KEMP. Chapters on Chaucer. Baltimore, Md.:
The Johns Hopkins Press; London: Oxford Univ Press,
1951.
A Griffith item (pp. 72-73); the following reviews should
be added to those listed by Griffith: Tauno F. Mustanoja,
NM, 54, 1953, 294-96; Howard R. Patch, MLN, 68, 1953,
553-57; Millett Henshaw, MLQ, 15, 1954, 273-74; D. S.
Bland, E Stud, 37, 1956, 78-81.
MASUI, MICHIO. The Language of Love in Chaucer. Studies
in English Literature (The English Literary Society of Ja-
pan), 1960, pp. 1-36.
----------. A Study of Chaucer. Tokyo: Kenkyusha, 1962.
MOGAN, JOSEPH JOHN, JR. Chaucer and the Theme of
Mutability. DA, 22, 3669-70. Louisiana State Univ, 1961.
MOSSÉ, FERNAND. Chaucer et le "Métier" de l'Écrivain.
EA, 7, 1954, 394-401.
MUSCATINE, CHARLES. Chaucer and the French Tradition:
A Study in Style and Meaning. Berkeley: Univ of California
Press; Cambridge Univ Press, 1957.
Rev: Robert O. Payne, CL, 9, 1957, 369-72; Paul G.
Ruggiers, BA, 32, 1958, 82; Hazard Adams, JA, 16,

1958, 534-35; J. Burke Severs, Spec, 33, 1958, 308-10;
Johannes Kleinstück, Ang, 75, 1957, 444-45; Joyce
Bazire, MLR, 53, 1958, 556-57; R. M. Wilson, Eng, 12,
1957, 61; J. Norton Smith, French Studies, 13, 1959, 57-
59; P. Mroczkowski, KN, No. 1, 1959, 64-67; Guy Bour-
quin, EA, 12, 1959, 60; John Burrow, EC, 10, 1960,
202-7; J. A. W. Bennett, RES, 12, 1961, 70.
PATCH, HOWARD R. On Rereading Chaucer. Harvard Univ
Press, 1959. 3rd printing.
   See Griffith, p. 74, for earlier printings and reviews.
----------, WALTER J. ONG, and HERBERT MARSHALL
McLUHAN. Christian Humanism in Letters. (The Mc-
Auley Lectures, 2nd Series, 1954.) West Hartford, Conn.:
St. Joseph College, 1955.
   Patch's lecture is entitled The Individual and the Type
in Medieval Literature.
PAYNE, ROBERT O. The Key of Remembrance: A Study of
Chaucer's Poetics. New Haven and London: Yale Univ
Press for the Univ of Cincinnati, 1963.
PECK, RUSSELL ALBERT. Number Symbolism and the
Idea of Order in the Works of Geoffrey Chaucer. DA, 24,
2894-95. Univ of Indiana, 1963.
PETER, JOHN. Complaint and Satire in Early English Liter-
ature. London: Oxford Univ Press, 1956.
   References to Chaucer as a satirist.
PRATT, ROBERT A. The New Century Cyclopedia of Names.
3 vols. New York: Appleton-Century-Crofts; London:
Bailey Brothers and Swinfen, 1954.
   Four entries deal with Chaucer: The Canterbury Tales
(p. 800); Geoffrey Chaucer (p. 917); The Legend of Good
Women (p. 2419); Troilus and Criseyde (p. 3905).
PRESTON, RAYMOND. Chaucer. New York: Sheed and
Ward, 1952; New York: Humanities Press, 1961 (reprint).
   A Griffith item (p. 75); the following reviews should be
added to those listed by Griffith: Marie P. Hamilton, AQ,
9, 1953, 354-57; List, 49, 1953, 193; Howard R. Patch,
MLN, 69, 1954, 371-74; Beverly Boyd, CW, 176, 1954,
318.
RENOIR, ALAIN. A Note on Chaucer's Women. NQ, 5, 1958,
283-84.

Descriptive passages in Chaucer and in the Metamorphoses (II, x) of Apuleius.

----------. Tradition and Moral Realism: Chaucer's Conception of the Poet. SN, 35, 1963, 199-210.

RICHARDSON, LILLA JANETTE. Irony Through Imagery: A Chaucerian Technique Studied in Relation to Sources, Analogues, and the Dicta of Medieval Rhetoric. DA, 24, 1176-77. Univ of California at Berkeley, 1962.

ROBERTSON, D. W. JR. A Preface to Chaucer: Studies in Medieval Perspectives. Princeton, N. J.: Princeton Univ Press; London: Oxford Univ Press, 1962.
  Rev: R. E. Kaske, Chaucer and Medieval Allegory, ELH, 30, 1963, 175-92; Brinley Rhys, A Preface to Chaucer, Sewanee Rev, 72, 1964, 335-41.

ROOT, R. K. The Poetry of Chaucer. Gloucester, Mass: Peter Smith, 1957.
  A reissue of the rev. 2nd ed. (1922); see Griffith, p. 76, for notice and reviews of the original ed. (1906).

ROWLAND, BERYL W. "Blyndes bestes": Aspects of Chaucer's Animal World. Unpub. Doct. Diss., Univ of British Columbia, 1962.

----------. Chaucer and the Unnatural History of Animals. Med Stud, 25, 1963, 367-72.

SALTER, F. M. Medieval Drama in Chester. Toronto: Univ of Toronto Press, 1955.
  References to Chaucer.

SAVAGE, HENRY LYTTLETON. The Gawain-Poet: Studies in His Personality and Background. Chapel Hill: Univ of North Carolina Press, 1956.
  Esp. Chapter i et passim.

SCHAAR, CLAES. Some Types of Narrative in Chaucer's Poetry. (Lund Studies in English, 25.) Lund: Gleerup; Copenhagen: Munksgaard, 1954.
  Rev: Kemp Malone, Spec, 31, 1956, 407-8; Gardiner Stillwell, JEGP, 54, 1955, 409-12; J. A. W. B(ennett), MAE, 25, 1956, 57-59.

----------. The Golden Mirror: Studies in Chaucer's Descriptive Technique and Its Literary Background. (Skrifter utgivna av Kungl. Humanistiska vetenskapssamfunder i Lund, 54.) Lund: Gleerup, 1955.

Rev: Nils Erik Enkvist, SN, 28, 1956, 257-58; Howard
R. Patch, MLN, 72, 1957, 540-42; D. S. Brewer, MLR,
52, 1957, 407-8; Ursula Brown, RES, 9, 1958, 297-300;
J. Norton Smith, MAE, 27, 1958, 43-44; Ruth Crosby,
Spec, 34, 1959, 326-29; Robert Worth Frank, Jr., JEGP,
59, 1960, 271-73; D. S. Bland, E Stud, 42, 1961, 98-100.
----------. A Postscript to Chaucer Studies. E Stud, 42
1961, 153-56.
A reply to critical reviews of the two books listed above
by Schaar.
SCHERER, JUDITH EMILY. The Staging of Reality: Tone
and Point of View in Chaucer. Univ of Rochester Diss.,
1959.
SCHLAUCH, MARGARET. English Medieval Literature and
Its Social Foundations. Warszawa: Panstwowe Wydawnic-
two Naukowe, 1956.
Chapter xi (Geoffrey Chaucer: Life and Earlier Works)
and Chapter xii (Chaucer's Canterbury Tales).
SCHOECK, RICHARD J., and JEROME TAYLOR, Eds.
Chaucer Criticism. Vol. I: The Canterbury Tales: Vol. II:
Troilus and Criseyde and The Minor Poems. Notre Dame,
Ind.: Univ of Notre Dame Press, 1960 and 1961.
The thirty-three essays in this two volume collection
are, with two exceptions, reprinted in slightly revised
form from journals. The two articles which appear for
the first time in this collection are noted in the appropriate
section of this bibliography. For similar collections of
essays, see Charles A. Owen (Discussions of the Canter-
bury Tales) in section entitled Canterbury Tales: General
and Edward C. Wagenknecht (Chaucer: Modern Essays in
Criticism) below in this section.
Rev (for Vol. I): R. W. Burchfield, NQ, 8, 1961, 242;
A. C. Cawley, MLR, 56, 1961, 466.
SCHMIDT-HIDDING, WOLFGANG. Sieben Meister des
Literarischen Humors in England und Amerika. Heidelberg: Quelle and Meyer, 1959.
SLAUGHTER, EUGENE EDWARD. Virtue According to
Love--in Chaucer. (Bookman Monograph Series for Mod-
ern Language Studies.) New York: Bookman Associates,
1957.

Rev: Claude E. Jones, BB, 22, 1958, 79; D. W. Robert-
son, Jr., MLN, 74, 1959, 60-61.
SMITH, R. B. A Note on Chaucer's Obscenity. CEA, 23,
1961, 6.
SPEIRS, JOHN. Chaucer the Maker. 2nd rev. ed. London:
Faber and Faber, 1960.
The 1st ed. (1951) is noted and reviews listed in Grif-
fith, p. 77; to these reviews of the 1st ed. should be added
the review by John Conley, Spec, 28, 1953, 200-2.
----------. Medieval English Poetry: The Non-Chaucerian
Tradition. London: Faber and Faber, 1957.
STAMBUSKY, ALAN A. Chaucer and Molière: Kindred Pat-
terns of the Dramatic Impulse in Human Comedy. Lock
Haven Review, Ser. 1, No. 5, 1963, 43-60.
STAVROU, C. N. Some Implications of Chaucer's Irony.
SAQ, 56, 1957, 454-61.
TAYLOR, JEROME. Oral Reading in the Teaching of Chau-
cer. CE, 19, 1958, 304-6.
TORNWALL, WILLIAM ALLEN. Studies in Chaucer's Image-
ry. DA, 16, 1676. Louisiana State Univ, 1956.
TURNELL, MARTIN. Belief and the Writer. The Common-
weal, 62, May 13, 1955, 143-46. See also the letters in
response to this article by C. Jessey, 257 (June 10), M.
Novak, 280-81 (June 17), M. Turnell, 331-32 (July 1),
J. J. Greene, 400-1 (July 22), and M. Novak, 518-19
(Aug 26).
UENO, NAOZO. The Religious View of Chaucer in His Italian Period. Tokyo: Nanundo, 1958.
WAGENKNECHT, EDWARD C., Ed. Chaucer: Modern Essays in Criticism. (A Galaxy Book, GB24.) New York:
Oxford Univ Press, 1959.
A reprint (with occasional revision) of twenty-six essays
which appeared, for the most part, in journals. The date
of the earliest article (G. L. Kittredge, Chaucer's Pardoner) is 1893; the date of the most recent is 1955. For
similar collections of essays, see Charles A. Owen (Discussions of the Canterbury Tales) in section Canterbury
Tales: General, and Richard J. Schoeck and Jerome Taylor (Chaucer Criticism, 2 vols.) above in this section.

Rev: Bernice M. Delaney, NMQ, 30, 1960, 97; Rosemary Woolf, CQ, 2, 1960, 192.
WILSON, HERMAN PLEDGER. Chaucer as a Prose Writer. DA, 16, 2154. Univ of Tennessee, 1956.
WRENN, C. L. On the Continuity of English Poetry. Ang, 76, 1958, 41-59.
For Chaucer, see pp. 47-51, et passim.
ZANCO, AURELIO. Chaucer e il suo mondo. Turin: G. B. Petrini, 1955.
ZESMER, DAVID M. Guide to English Literature: From Beowulf through Chaucer and Medieval Drama. (College Outline Series, 53.) New York: Barnes and Noble, 1961.
Discussion and summary of Chaucer's works, pp. 190-259; annotated bibliography for Chaucer, pp. 353-74, compiled by Stanley B. Greenfield.

LITERARY RELATIONS AND SOURCES

See Griffith, pp. 81-99.

AIKEN, PAULINE. Vincent of Beauvais and the "Houres" of Chaucer's Physician. SP, 53, 1956, 22-24.

BAUGH, ALBERT C. Chaucer and the Panthère d'Amours. Britannica: Festschrift für Hermann M. Flasdieck, pp. 51-61. Heidelberg: Winter: Universitäts-verlag, 1960.

BEVINGTON, DAVID M. On Translating Ovid in Chaucer's House of Fame. NQ, 7, 1960, 206-7.

BOSSUAT, R. Le Roman de Renard. Paris: Hatier-Boivin, 1957.

BRATCHER, JAMES T. A Chaucer Analogue in Spanish-American Tradition. NQ, 10, 1963, 210-12.
    An analogue of the Miller's Tale in the writings of Juan B. Rael.

BRYAN, W. F., and GERMAINE DEMPSTER. Sources and Analogues of Chaucer's Canterbury Tales. New York: Humanities Press; London: Routledge and Kegan Paul, 1958.
    A reissue of the 1st ed. (1941); see Griffith, pp. 82-83, for reviews.

CHIARENZA, FRANK JOHN. Chaucer and the Medieval Amorous Complaint. Unpub. Doct. Diss., Yale Univ, 1956.

CLOGAN, PAUL MAURICE. Chaucer and the Medieval Statius. DA, 22, 3641. Univ of Illinois, 1961.

CRAIG, HARDIN. From Gorgias to Troilus. Pp. 97-107 in
Studies in Medieval Literature: In Honor of Professor
Albert Croll Baugh, edited by MacEdward Leach. Phila-
delphia: Univ of Pennsylvania Press; London: Oxford Univ
Press, 1961.
DAHLBERG, CHARLES R. Macrobius and the Unity of the
Roman de la Rose. SP, 58, 1961, 573-82.
DEAN, RUTH J. The Manuscripts of Nicholas Trevet's
Anglo-Norman Chronicles. M and H, Fasc. 14, 1962,
pp. 95-105.
DÉDÉYAN, CHARLES. Dante en Angleterre. Les Lettres
Romanes, 12, 1958, 367-88; 13, 1959, 45-68.
     The serial publication of this monograph is continued
through Vol. XV, 1961; only the portion dealing with Dante
and Chaucer is listed above.
DONOVAN, MORTIMER J. The Anticlaudian and Three Pas-
sages in the Franklin's Tale. JEGP, 56, 1957, 52-59.
FISH, STANLEY E. The Nun's Priest's Tale and Its Ana-
logues. CLAJ, 5, 1962, 223-28.
FOSTER, KENELM. Italy and the English Poets: Chaucer,
Dante and Boccaccio. The Tablet, 206, 1955, 476-77.
FRIEND, ALBERT C. The Proverbs of Serlo of Wilton. Med
Stud, 16, 1954, 179-218.
----------. Analogues in Cheriton to the Pardoner and His
Sermon. JEGP, 53, 1954, 383-88.
     Notes parallels from the sermons of Odo of Cheriton
(d. 1245-46).
GREEN, RICHARD HAMILTON. Classical Fable and English
Poetry in the Fourteenth Century. Critical Approaches to
Medieval Literature, pp. 110-33.
     For a description of this collection of essays, see
section General Criticism under the name of the editor,
Dorothy Bethurum.
----------. Alan of Lille's De planctu Naturae. Spec, 31,
1956, 649-74.
     No direct reference to Chaucer.
HALL, LOUIS BREWER. Chaucer and the Dido-and-Aeneas
Story. Med Stud, 25, 1963, 148-59.
HARDER, KELSIE B. Chaucer's Use of the Mystery Plays
in the Miller's Tale. MLQ, 17, 1956, 193-98.

HARTUNG, ALBERT EDWARD. A Study of the Textual Affiliations of Chaucer's Melibeus Considered in Its Relation
to the French Source. DA, 17, 2259-60. Lehigh Univ,
1957.

HAZLETON, RICHARD MARQUAND. Two Texts of the Disticha Catonis and Its Commentary, with Special Reference
to Chaucer, Langland, and Gower. DA, 16, 1899. Rutgers
Univ, 1956.

----------. The Christianization of "Cato": the Disticha Catonis in the Light of Late Mediaeval Commentaries. Med
Stud, 19, 1957, 157-73.
    Extensive footnote bibliographies.

----------. Chaucer and Cato. Spec, 35, 1960, 357-80.

----------. Chaucer's Parson's Tale and the Moralium Dogma Philosophorum. Traditio, 16, 1960, 255-74.

HINTON, NORMAN DEXTER. A Study of the Medieval English Poems Relating the Destruction of Troy. DA, 17,
2010-11. Univ of Wisconsin, 1957.

ISAACS, NEIL D. Constance in Fourteenth-Century England.
NM, 59, 1958, 260-77.
    Comparison of the Constance story in Chaucer and in
Gower and in Emare.

KELLOGG, ALFRED L. Chaucer's Self-Portrait and Dante's. MAE, 29, 1960, 119-20.

KINNEY, THOMAS LEROY. English Verse of Complaint,
1250-1400. DA, 20, 1767-68. Univ of Michigan, 1959.

KREUZER, JAMES R. An Alleged Crux in Chaucer. NQ, 4,
1957, 409.
    Chaucer's Lollius; see article by W. Morel, below in
this section.

LEACH, ELEANOR JANE WINSOR. The Sources and Rhetoric of Chaucer's Legend of Good Women and Ovid's
Heroides. Yale Univ Diss., 1963.

LEWIS, R. W. B. On Translating the Aeneid: "Yif That I
Can." Yearbook of Comparative and General Literature
(Univ of North Carolina Studies in Comparative Litera-
ture), 10, 1961, 7-15.
    HF, 143.

LUMIANSKY, R. M. Calchas in the Early Versions of the
Troilus Story. TSE, 4, 1954, 5-20.

The character and function of Calchas in Benoît de
Sainte-Maure, Guido de Columna, Boccaccio, and Chau-
cer.
----------. The Story of Troilus and Briseida According to
Benoît and Guido. Spec, 29, 1954, 727-33.
----------. Aspects of the Relationship of Boccaccio's Il
Filostrato with Benoît's Roman de Troie and Chaucer's
Wife of Bath's Tale. Italica, 31, 1954, 1-7.
----------. Benoît's Portraits and Chaucer's General Pro-
logue. JEGP, 55, 1956, 431-38.
----------. The Story of Troilus and Briseida in the Laud
Troy-Book. MLQ, 18, 1957, 238-46.
----------. Structural Unity in Benoît's Roman de Troie.
Rom, 79, 1958, 410-24.
MAGOUN, FRANCIS P., JR. Chaucer's Summary of Statius'
Thebaid II-XII. Traditio, 11, 1955, 409-20.
MAKAREWICZ, SISTER MARY RAYNELDA. The Patristic
Influence on Chaucer. The Catholic Univ of America
Press, 1953.
    See Griffith, p. 91, for the listing of this work as a
doctoral dissertation.
MATTHEWS, WILLIAM. Eustache Deschamps and Chaucer's
Merchant's Tale. MLR, 51, 1956, 217-20.
MOREL, W. An Alleged Crux in Chaucer. NQ, 4, 1957,
238-39.
    Chaucer's Lollius; see article by James R. Kreuzer,
above in this section.
MORETON, REBECCA LARCHE. Literary Convention in
The Book of the Duchess. UMSE, 4, 1963, 69-78.
MUSCATINE, CHARLES. Chaucer and the French Tradition:
A Study in Style and Meaning. Berkeley: Univ of California
Press; Cambridge Univ Press, 1957.
    See section General Criticism for numerous reviews of
this book.
OLSON, PAUL A. Le Jaloux and History: A Study in Medi-
aeval Comic Convention. DA, 19, 2603. Princeton Univ,
1957.
PRATT, ROBERT A. Chaucer and Le Roman de Troyle et
de Criseida. SP, 53, 1956, 509-39.

Contends that Chaucer's chief source for the Troilus is
not Boccaccio but a French translation of Il Filostrato
made by one Beauvau, Seneschal of Anjou.

----------. Chaucer and Isidore on Why Men Marry. MLN,
74, 1959, 293-94.

Isidore of Seville's Etymologiarum Libri XX, IX, vii,
29 as possible source for WBPro, 257-62.

PRAZ, MARIO. The Flaming Heart: Essays on Crashaw,
Machiavelli, and Other Studies of the Relations Between
Italian and English Literature from Chaucer to T. S. El-
iot. Garden City: Doubleday, 1958.

See Chapter entitled Chaucer and the Great Italian Writers of the Trecento.

Rev: Chandler B. Beall, CL, 10, 1958, 358-60.

RENOIR, ALAIN. Another Minor Analogue to Chaucer's
Pandarus. NQ, 5, 1958, 421-22.

Compares Pandarus with Spurius, the pander, in Alda,
a twelfth century Latin farce by Guillaume de Blois.

RUGGIERS, PAUL G. Words into Images in Chaucer's Hous
of Fame: A Third Suggestion. MLN, 69, 1954, 34-37.

HF, 1068-81, and Paradiso, Canto 3.

SCHLESS, HOWARD. Chaucer and Dante: A Revaluation.
DA, 16, 1675. Univ of Pennsylvania, 1956.

----------. Chaucer and Dante. Critical Approaches to
Medieval Literature, pp. 134-54.

For a description of this collection of essays, see
section General Criticism under the name of the editor,
Dorothy Bethurum.

SELLS, A. LYTTON. The Italian Influence in English Poetry
from Chaucer to Southwell. Bloomington, Ind.: Univ of
Indiana Press, 1955.

SILVIA, DANIEL SHIVER, JR. Chaucer's Use of Jerome's
Adversus Jovinianum, with an Edition of Book I, Chapters
40-49, Based on a Study of Medieval Manuscripts. DA,
23, 4345-46. Univ of Illinois, 1962.

SOLARI, M. S. Sources of the Invocation in the House of
Fame. Revista de Literaturas Modernas (Mendoza, Ar-
gentina), No. 1, 1956 (pub. 1957), 217-25.

STEADMAN, JOHN M. The Book-Burning Episode in the

Wife of Bath's Prologue: Some Additional Analogues.
PMLA, 74, 1959, 521-25.
----------. The Prioress's Tale and "Granella" of Para-
diso. Med Stud, 24, 1962, 388-91.
STIGALL, JOHN O. The Manuscript Tradition of the De Vita
et Moribus Philosophorum of Walter Burley. M and H,
Fasc. 11, 1957, pp. 44-57.
    Suggests that the De Vita was used by Chaucer as "a
source in the Canterbury Tales."
STILLWELL, GARDINER. The Language of Love in Chau-
cer's Miller's and Reeve's Tales and in the Old French
Fabliaux. JEGP, 54, 1955, 693-99.
SUTHERLAND, RONALD. The Romaunt of the Rose and
Source Manuscripts. PMLA, 74, 1959, 178-83.
THOMPSON, W. MEREDITH. Chaucer's Translation of the
Bible. English and Medieval Studies: Presented to J. R. R.
Tolkien on the Occasion of His Seventieth Birthday, pp.
183-99. Edited by Norman Davis and C₀ L. Wrenn. Lon-
don: George Allen and Unwin, 1962.
THOMSON, PATRICIA. The "Canticus Troili": Chaucer and
Petrarch. CL, 11, 1959, 313-28.
UTLEY, FRANCIS LEE. The Study of Folk Literature: Its
Scope and Use. JAF, 71, 1958, 139-48.
    Not directly concerned with Chaucer; a description of
the aims and methods of the Folklorist.
----------. Folk Literature: An Operational Definition.
JAF, 74, 1961, 193-206.
WENK, J. C. On the Sources of the Prioress's Tale. Med
Stud, 17, 1955, 214-19.
    Influence of the liturgy for the Feast of the Holy Inno-
cents upon the imagery of the PriorT.
WILKINSON, LANCELOT PATRICK. Ovid Recalled. Cam-
bridge Univ Press, 1955.
    See esp. Chapter xi: The Middle Ages: Venus' Clerk
Ovyde.
WRIGHT, HERBERT GLADSTONE. Boccaccio in England
from Chaucer to Tennyson. London: Athlone Press, 1957.
    Rev: TLS, July 11, 1958, 458; D. S. Brewer, MAE,
28, 1959, 68-69.

INFLUENCE AND ALLUSIONS

See Griffith, pp. 100-16.

ALDERSON, WILLIAM L. On Two Chaucer Allusions. MLN, 71, 1956, 166-67.
    See the articles by John Owen and Philip Williams, below in this section.

APPLEMAN, PHILIP. Another Modernized Shipman's Tale. CE, 18, 1956, 168-69.

AYRES, ROBERT W. Medieval History, Moral Purpose, and the Structure of Lydgate's Siege of Thebes. PMLA, 73, 1958, 463-74.

BLENNER-HASSETT, ROLAND. Yeats' Use of Chaucer. Ang, 72, 1954, 455-62.

BOWERS, R. H. Impingham's Borrowings from Chaucer. MLN, 73, 1958, 327-29.

----------. Chaucer's Troilus as an Elizabethan Wanton Book. NQ, 7, 1960, 370-71.

BOYD, BEVERLY. The Literary Background of Lydgate's The Legend of Dan Joos. MLN, 72, 1957, 81-87.
    Lydgate and Chaucer's PriorT.

BRADBROOK, M. C. What Shakespeare Did to Chaucer's Troilus and Criseyde. SQ, 9, 1958, 311-19.

BURGESS, C. F. Gay's 'Twas When the Seas Were Roaring,' and Chaucer's Franklin's Tale: A Borrowing. NQ, 9, 1962, 454-55.

BUXTON, JOHN. Elizabethan Taste. London: Macmillan, 1963.
Chapter vi (pp. 221-30): Literature: The Elizabethan Appreciation of Chaucer.

CAMDEN, CARROLL. Chaucer and Two Elizabethan Pseudo-Sciences. PQ, 38, 1959, 124-26.

CAUTHEN, I. B., JR. Another Chaucer Allusion in Harsnet (1603). NQ, 5, 1958, 248-49.

COGHILL, NEVILL. Shakespeare's Reading in Chaucer. Pp. 86-99 in Elizabethan and Jacobean Studies Presented to Frank Percy Wilson in Honour of His Seventieth Birthday. Oxford: Clarendon Press, 1959.

COHEN, HENNIG. An Early American Chaucer Allusion. NQ, 5, 1958, 245.
A commendatory poem by Ward in Anne Bradstreet's Tenth Muse.

d'ARDENNE, S. R. T. O. Troilus and Criseyde and The Tragic Comedians. E Stud, 44, 1963, 12-19.
Chaucer's poem and Meredith's novel.

DOBBINS, AUSTIN C. Chaucer Allusions: 1619-1732. MLQ, 18, 1957, 309-12.

----------. Dryden's "Character of a Good Parson": Background and Interpretation. SP, 53, 1956, 51-59.
"Dryden's imitative version of Chaucer's 'poore Parson of a toun.'"

DODDS, M. H. What is Chaucer's Borrow? NQ, 3, 1956, 317-18.
A reply to a question posed earlier by Lisle C. John; see below in this section for the article by John.

EMERSON, FRANCIS WILLARD. The Bible in Spenser's Chaucer. NQ, 5, 1958, 422-23.

----------. The Spenser-Followers in Leigh Hunt's Chaucer. NQ, 5, 1958, 284-86.

EMERSON, KATHERINE T. A Chaucer Borrowing in Kristin Lavransdatter. NQ, 2, 1955, 370-71.

EVANS, MAURICE. English Poetry in the Sixteenth Century. London: Hutchinson's University Library, 1955.

FRANK, JOSEPH. An Early Newspaper Reference to Chaucer. NQ, 3, 1956, 298.

FREEMAN, ARTHUR. A Note on George Wither. NQ, 7, 1960, 407-8.

----------. Richard II, I. iii. 294-95. SQ, 14, 1963, 89-90.
Cites Coghill for noting parallel between these lines in Richard II and WBT, 1139-40;see reply by J. C. Maxwell below in this section.

GESNER, CAROL. A Note on Henry Vaughan. MLR, 50, 1955, 172-73.

GREEN, DAVID B. A Chaucer Allusion in Edward DuBois' Old Nick. NQ, 1, 1954, 417.

GRENNEN, JOSEPH E. Chaucer in a Chapel Perilous: The Waste Land, 1-18 and 230-42. English Record, 13, 1962, 38-39.

HARDISON, O. B., JR., Ed. William Caxton: Preface to the Canterbury Tales. Pp. 18-20 of English Literary Criticism: The Renaissance. New York: Appleton-Century-Crofts, 1963.

HUSSEY, DYNELEY. Walton's Troilus and Cressida. Music and Letters, 36, 1955, 139-45.
Review of Sir William Walton's opera based on Chaucer's Troilus.

JOHN, LISLE C. What is Chaucer's Borrow? NQ, 3, 1956, 97-98.
For a reply to this query, see M. H. Dodds, above in this section.

KINGHORN, A. M. The Mediaeval Makars. TSLL, 1, 1959, 73-88.
This article is concerned with the precise nature of the indebtedness of the Scots poets of the fifteenth and sixteenth centuries to Chaucer.

----------. Warton's History and Early English Poetry. E Stud, 44, 1963, 197-204.

LANGSTON, BEACH. William Penn and Chaucer. NQ, 1, 1954, 49-50.

LAVIN, J. A. The Clerk of Oxenford in Oral Tradition. New York Folklore Quarterly, 17, 1961, 61-64.

LILL, JAMES VERNON. Dryden's Adaptations from Milton, Shakespeare, and Chaucer. DA, 14, 1214. Univ of Minnesota, 1954.

LOBZOWSKA, MARIA. Two English Translations of the

XVth Century French Satire Les Quinze Joyes de Mari-
age. KN, 10, 1963, 17-32.
  Chaucerian echoes in English translations of the French
  text.
MACKERNESS, E. D. Two Chaucer Allusions of 1659. NQ,
5, 1958, 197-98; reprinted, 245-46.
MAVEETY, STANLEY R. Hermione, A Dangerous Orna-
ment. SQ, 14, 1963, 485-86.
  When Leontes speaks of his "dagger muzzled" (The
  Winter's Tale I, ii, 156), the reference "is a conscious
  echoing of a proverb recorded in English as early as
  Chaucer" (MerT, 1839).
MAXWELL, J. C. Chaucer in the Queen Mab Speech. NQ,
7, 1960, 16.
  Suggests PF as source for Romeo and Juliet, I, iv,
  70-88.
----------. Richard II, I, iii, 294-95. SQ, 14, 1963, 283.
  A reply to Arthur Freeman; see above in this section.
MORAN, TATYANA. The Meeting of the Lovers in the Tes-
tament of Cresseid. NQ, 10, 1963, 11-12.
MUSCATINE, CHARLES. The Book of Geoffrey Chaucer:
An Account of the Publication of Geoffrey Chaucer's Works
from the Fifteenth Century to Modern Times. San Fran-
cisco: The Book Club of California, 1963. Illustrated;
limited ed.
OWEN, CHARLES A., JR. The Canterbury Tales: Early
Manuscripts and Relative Popularity. JEGP, 54, 1955,
104-10.
OWEN, JOHN. A Euphemistic Allusion to the Reeve's Tale.
MLN, 69, 1954, 43-44.
PARKS, EDD WINFIELD. Hayne's Adaptation of Chaucer's
Franklin's Tale. Essays in Honor of Walter Clyde Curry,
pp. 103-15. Nashville, Tenn.: Vanderbilt Univ Press,
1954.
PEARCE, T. M. "Another Knot, Five-Finger-Tied": Shake-
speare's Troilus and Cressida, V, ii, 157. NQ, 7, 1960,
18-19.
  Chaucer's ParsT may have served as source for Shake-
  speare's image.
PETTIGREW, RICHARD D. Die One, Die Three (On the

Passing of Mrs. Gamp, the Wife of Bath, and Juliet's
Nurse). CE, 19, 1957-58, 80.
   Poem.
PIERCE, MARVIN. Another Chaucer Allusion: 1672. NQ,
   4, 1957, 2-3.
PLUMSTEAD, A. W. Satirical Parody in Roister Doister:
   A Reinterpretation. SP, 60, 1963, 141-54.
   Echoes of Chaucer's Troilus in Nicholas Udall's play.
PRESSON, ROBERT K. The Conclusion of Love's Labour's
   Lost. NQ, 7, 1960, 17-18.
   Suggests that Shakespeare is indebted to PF for the end-
   ing of Love's Labour's Lost.
RANDALL, DALE B. J. A 1613 Chaucer Allusion. PQ, 39,
   1960, 131-32.
RENOIR, ALAIN. Chaucerian Character Names in Lydgate's
   Siege of Thebes. MLN, 71, 1956, 249-56.
----------. John Lydgate: Poet of the Transition. EM, 11,
   1960, 9-19.
RUFFIN, DAVID. Browning's Childe Roland and Chaucer's
   House of Fame. Essays in Honor of Walter Clyde Curry,
   pp. 51-60. Nashville, Tenn.: Vanderbilt Univ Press,
   1954.
SCHANZER, ERNEST. Antony and Cleopatra and The Leg-
   end of Good Women. NQ, 7, 1960, 335-36.
SCHLAUCH, MARGARET. Troilus i Kressyda Szekspira
   i Chaucera---Jezyk Metaforyczny w Swietle Przemian
   Spolecznych. KN, 1, 1954, 3-19.
   A contrast of the poem and the play, particularly in
   terms of social and economic changes as these are re-
   flected in the imagery.
SHERBO, ARTHUR. Fielding and Chaucer--and Smart.
   NQ, 5, 1958, 441-42.
SINGER, ARMAND E. Chaucer and Don Juan. West Virginia
   University Philological Papers, 13, Dec 1961 (pub. 1962),
   25-30.
SLOANE, WILLIAM. Chaucer, Milton, and the Rev. William
   Stukeley, M. D. NQ, 7, 1960, 220-22.
SMITH, J. NORTON. Lydgate's Changes in the Temple of
   Glas. MAE, 27, 1958, 166-72.
SPECTOR, R. D. Dryden's Translation of Chaucer: A

Problem in Neo-Classical Diction. NQ, 3, 1956, 23-26.
SPURGEON, CAROLINE F. Five Hundred Years of Chaucer
Criticism and Allusion, 1357-1900. 3 vols, reissued.
New York: Russell and Russell, 1961.
    See Griffith, p. 112, for reviews of 1st ed.; for review
of this reprint, see John Burrow, CQ, 3, 1961, 283-84.
STROUD, THEODORE A. Chaucer's Shipman's Tale in Mod-
ern Dress. CE, 17, 1955, 109-10.
STROUP, THOMAS B. George Daniel: Cavalier Poet. Ren-
aissance Papers, 1957, 39-51.
    References to Chaucer in Daniel.
WAGGONER, GEORGE R. Allusions to Chaucer in Stow's
Summarye of the Chronicles of England, 1570. NQ, 3,
1956, 462.
WILLIAMS, PHILIP. A 1593 Chaucer Allusion. MLN, 69,
1954, 45.
WOOLF, HENRY BOSLEY. Review of Laurence Nowell's
Vocabularium Saxonicum. MLN, 69, 1954, 288-89.
    A 1567 allusion to I (A) 236: . . . and pleyen on a rote.
ZIMANSKY, CURT A., Ed. The Critical Works of Thomas
Rymer. New Haven: Yale Univ Press, 1956.
    Some seventeenth-century views of Chaucer's language.

STYLE
INCLUDING VERSIFICATION AND PUNS

See Griffith, pp. 116-127.

ANDERSON, RETA MARGARET. Some Functions of Medieval Rhetoric in Chaucer's Verse Narratives. Yale Univ Diss., 1963.

BAUM, PAULL F. Chaucer's Puns. PMLA, 71, 1956, 225-46.

----------. Chaucer's Puns: A Supplementary List. PMLA, 73, 1958, 167-70.

----------. Chaucer's Verse. Durham, N.C.: Duke Univ Press; Cambridge Univ Press, 1961.
Rev: Ewald Standop, Ang, 80, 1963, 448-53.

BECK, RICHARD J. Educational Expectation and Rhetorical Result in The Canterbury Tales. E Stud, 44, 1963, 241-53.

BEICHNER, PAUL E. Non Alleluia Ructare. Med Stud, 18, 1956, 135-44.
The pun on "eructare" in SumT, 1934: Lo, "buf!" they seye, "cor meum eructavit!"

BIGGINS, D(ENNIS). Chaucer's General Prologue, A163. NQ, 6, 1959, 435-36.
Additional support for Baum's suggestion (PMLA, 71, 1956) that GP, 673, contains a pun on the word "burdoun." See Miller, below in this section.

----------. More Chaucerian Ambiguities: A652, 664,
D1346. NQ, 9, 1962, 165-67.
>   Additions to Baum's lists.
BLOOMFIELD, MORTON W. Symbolism in Medieval Liter-
ature. MP, 56, 1958-59, 73-81.
----------. A Grammatical Approach to Personification Al-
legory. MP, 60, 1962-63, 161-71.
BREWER, D. S., and F. W. BATESON. English in the University: III. Language and Literature. EC, 11, 1961,
243-63.
>   In an Editorial Appendix (pp. 255-63) to the essay by
Brewer, F. W. Bateson discusses the question of style in
Chaucer's poetry and illustrates his remarks by stylistic
analysis of the first stanza of PF.
CLARK, DONALD LEMEN. Rhetoric and the Literature of
the English Middle Ages. QJS, 45, 1959, 19-28.
>   "Rhetoric did teach the poets, as well as the prose wri-
ters, to find arguments and to use an embellished and
copious style, as the allegories attest."
CURTIUS, ERNST ROBERT. European Literature and the
Latin Middle Ages. Trans. by Willard R. Trask. New
York: Pantheon Books for Bollingen Foundation (Bollingen
Series 36), 1953.
DEMPSTER, GERMAINE. Dramatic Irony in Chaucer. New
York: The Humanities Press, 1959.
>   A reissue of the ed. first published in 1932; see Griffith,
p. 119, for reviews.
DONAHUE, CHARLES. Patristic Exegesis in the Criticism
of Medieval Literature: Summation. Critical Approaches
to Medieval Literature, pp. 61-82.
>   For a description of this collection of essays, see
section General Criticism under the name of the editor,
Dorothy Bethurum.
DONALDSON, E. TALBOT. Patristic Exegesis in the Criti-
cism of Medieval Literature: The Opposition. Critical
Approaches to Medieval Literature, pp. 1-26.
>   See note to preceding entry.
ELIASON, NORMAN E. Some Word-Play in Chaucer's
Reeve's Tale. MLN, 71, 1956, 162-64.
ELLIOTT, RALPH W. V. Landscape and Rhetoric in

Middle-English Alliterative Poetry. Melbourne Critical
Review, 4, 1961, 65-76.
Some discussion of rhetoric in PF.
EVERETT, DOROTHY. Essays on Middle English Litera-
ture. Ed. by Patricia Kean. London: Oxford Univ Press,
1955.
Reprinted in this collection are two articles listed by
Griffith, p. 119: Chaucer's Good Ear and Some Reflections
on Chaucer's "Art Poetical. "
FARRELL, WILLIAM J. Chaucer's Use of the Catalogue.
TSLL, 5, 1963, 64-78.
FRIEDMAN, LIONEL J. Jean de Meung, Anti-feminism,
and Bourgeois Realism. MP, 57, 1959-60, 13-23.
GIFFIN, MARY. Studies on Chaucer and His Audience. Hull,
Quebec: Les Éditions l'Éclair, 1956.
See section entitled General Criticism for reviews.
GREEN, A. WIGFALL. Chaucer's Sir Thopas: Meter,
Rhyme, and Contrast. UMSE, 1, 1960, 1-11.
----------. Meter and Rhyme in Chaucer's Anelida and
Arcite. UMSE, 2, 1961, 55-63.
----------. Chaucer's Complaints: Stanzaic Arrangement,
Meter and Rhyme. UMSE, 3, 1962, 19-34.
GRIFFITH, PHILIP MAHONE. Chaucer's Merchant's Tale.
Expl, 16, 1957, Item 13.
Additional evidence in support of the contention by
William W. Main (below in this section) that MerT, 2257,
contains a pun on "lechour. "
HAGSTRUM, JEAN H. The Sister Arts: The Tradition of
Literary Pictorialism and English Poetry from Dryden to
Gray. Chicago: Univ of Chicago Press, 1958.
References to Chaucer.
HOWELL, WILBUR S. Logic and Rhetoric in England.
Princeton Univ Press, 1956.
References to Chaucer and rhetoric.
HUSEBOE, ARTHUR R. Chaucerian Puns on "Brotel. "
North Dakota Quarterly, 31, 1963, 35-37.
KASKE, R. E. Patristic Exegesis in the Criticism of Medi-
eval Literature: The Defense. Critical Approaches to
Medieval Literature, pp. 27-60.

For a description of this collection of essays, see
section General Criticism, under the name of the editor,
Dorothy Bethurum.

KEE, KENNETH. Two Chaucerian Gardens. Med Stud, 23,
1961, 154-62.
Chaucer's use of the rhetorical commonplaces of garden
description in MerT and FrankT.

KÖKERITZ, HELGE. Rhetorical Word-Play in Chaucer.
PMLA, 69, 1954, 937-52.

KORNBLUTH, ALICE FOX. Another Chaucer Pun. NQ, 6,
1959, 243.
T and C, IV, 312.

LANDRUM, GRAHAM G. An Interpretation of the Clerk's
Tale According to Mediaeval Literary Theory, Based on
a Study of Sources and Analogues. DA, 14, 1725. Princeton Univ, 1954.

McCALL, JOHN P. Medieval Exegesis: Some Documents for
the Literary Critic. Pp. 227-67 in Christ and Apollo: the
Dimensions of the Literary Imagination, edited by William
F. Lynch, New York: Sheed and Ward, 1960.
Twenty "documents" drawn from Medieval writers
(Hugh of St. Victor, St. Thomas, etc.) and from modern
critics (D. W. Robertson, Jr., Morton Bloomfield, etc.).

McCRACKEN, SAMUEL. Chaucer's Sir Thopas, B^2, 1914-
1915. Expl, 17, 1959, Item 57.
Suggests a pun on "doghty" in Sir Thopas, 724: Sire
Thopas wax a doghty swayn.

MAIN, WILLIAM W. Chaucer's The Merchant's Tale, 2257-
2261. Expl, 14, 1955, Item 13.
Pun upon "lechour" in MerT, 2257. See Griffith (above
in this section) for additional evidence.

MILLER, B. D. H. Chaucer's General Prologue, A 673:
Further Evidence. NQ, 7, 1960, 404-6.
Further evidence is cited (from de Meun and Deschamps)
in support of the pun on "burdoun" in GP, 673; see Baum
and Biggins, above in this section.

MROCZKOWSKI, PRZEMYSLAW. Mediaeval Art and Aesthetics in The Canterbury Tales. Spec, 33, 1958, 204-21.

MURPHY, JAMES JEROME. Chaucer, Gower, and the

English Rhetorical Tradition. DA, 17, 849-50. Stanford
Univ, 1957.
----------. The Earliest Teaching of Rhetoric at Oxford.
Speech Monographs, 27, 1960, 354-67.
----------. The Arts of Discourse, 1050-1400. Med Stud,
23, 1961, 194-205.
----------. John Gower's Confessio Amantis and the First
Discussion of Rhetoric in the English Language. PQ, 41,
1962, 401-11.
MUSCATINE, CHARLES. Chaucer and the French Tradition:
A Study in Style and Meaning. Berkeley: Univ of California
Press; Cambridge Univ Press, 1957.
    See section General Criticism for numerous reviews of
this book.
----------. Locus of Action in Medieval Narrative. Ro-
mance Philology, 17, 1963, 115-22.
    Gothic style in CT.
NYKROG, PER. Les Fabliaux: Étude d'Histoire Littéraire
et de Stylistique Médiévale. Copenhagen: Einar Munks-
gaard, 1957.
    Rev: Charles H. Livingston, Spec, 33, 1958, 310-16.
PARR, ROGER PHILLIP. The Rhetorical Tradition and
Chaucer's Narrative Technique. Univ of Toronto Diss.,
1956.
PAYNE, ROBERT O. The Key of Remembrance: A Study of
Chaucer's Poetics. New Haven and London: Yale Univ
Press for the Univ of Cincinnati, 1963.
    See esp. Chapter i (The Rhetorical Tradition) and
Chapter ii (Chaucer on the Art of Poetry).
ROBERTSON, D. W., JR. A Preface to Chaucer: Studies
in Medieval Perspectives. Princeton, N.J.: Princeton
Univ Press; London: Oxford Univ Press, 1962.
    Illustrated with 118 plates; see section General Criti-
cism for reviews.
SHAIN, CHARLES E. Pulpit Rhetoric in Three Canterbury
Tales. MLN, 70, 1955, 235-45.
    Pulpit rhetoric in PardT, SumT and MerT.
SOUTHWORTH, JAMES G. Verses of Cadence: An Intro-
duction to the Prosody of Chaucer and His Followers.
Oxford: Basil Blackwell, 1954.

Rev: D. S. Brewer, RES, 6, 1955, 303-4; Kemp
Malone, Ang, 78, 1960, 238-40.
----------. The Prosody of Chaucer and His Followers.
Oxford: Basil Blackwell, 1962.
SPEARING, A. C. The Testament of Cresseid and the "High
Concise Style." Spec, 37, 1962, 208-25.
STEADMAN, JOHN M. Simkin's Camus Nose: A Latin Pun
in the Reeve's Tale? MLN, 75, 1960, 4-8.
STRODE, LENA VIRGINIA. A Study of Descriptive Tech-
niques in Narrative Poetry from Chaucer to Milton. DA,
23, 228. Univ of Denver, 1961.
TOWNSEND, JAMES ELBERT, JR. Chaucer's Lyricism: A
Study in Viewpoint and Structure. Univ of California Diss.,
1957.
WHITELEY, M. Verse and Its Feet. RES, 9, 1958, 268-79.
Criticism of F. T. Prince's The Italian Element in
Milton's Verse (Oxford, 1954); in the discussion examples
from Chaucer are subjected to analysis.

LANGUAGE AND WORD STUDY

See Griffith, pp. 128-42; 143-50.

For PUNS, see preceding section: STYLE.

BAKER, DONALD C. Gold Coins in English Mediaeval Lit-
erature. Spec, 36, 1961, 282-87.
"Most of the literary illustrations will be drawn from
Chaucer for the obvious reason of his general availability.
The coins for discussion are the florin, noble, écu, mou-
ton d'or, and ducat. "

BENNETT, JOSEPHINE WATERS. The Mediaeval Loveday.
Spec, 33, 1958, 351-70.
GP, 258-61; HF, 695-96.

BENSON, L. D. Chaucer's Historical Present: Its Meaning
and Uses. E Stud, 42, 1961, 65-77.

BERNDT, ROLF. Einführung in das Studium des Mittelenglischen unter Zugrundlegung des Prologs der Canterbury Tales. Halle/Salle: Niemeyer, 1960.
General discussion of Middle English; detailed glossary
of words which appear in GP.

BLOOMFIELD, MORTON W. Middle English "Gladly, " an
Instance of Linguisticism. NM, 63, 1962, 167-74.

BROOKE-ROSE, CHRISTINE. A Grammar of Metaphor.

London: Secker and Warburg, 1958; Chester Springs, Pa.:
Dufour, 1959.

See esp. pp. 289-91 et passim.

BRUNNER, KARL. Abriss der mittelenglischen Grammatik.
5th ed. Tübingen: Niemeyer Verlag, 1962.

See Griffith, p. 129, for notice of 1st ed. (1938).

----------. An Outline of Middle English Grammar. Trans.
by G. K. W. Johnston. Cambridge, Mass.: Harvard Univ
Press, 1963.

DENT, A. A. Chaucer and the Horse. Leeds, 9, 1959, 1-12.
Deals with the technical vocabulary used by Chaucer to
describe horses, riding equipment, etc.; illustrated.

DONALDSON, E. TALBOT. Chaucer's Miller's Tale,
A 3483-86. MLN, 69, 1954, 310-13.
Proposes the reading "nerye" (from OE nerian) in place
of the reading "verye" which appears in line 3485 in most
editions.

ETHEL, GARLAND. Horse or Horses: A Chaucerian Textual
Problem. MLN, 75, 1960, 97-101.
Suggests that "were" in GP 74 (His hors were goode),is
subjunctive and its subject singular. For reply see W. H.
French, below in this section.

FINKENSTAEDT, THOMAS. You and Thou: Studien zur
Anrede im Englischen (mit einem Exkurs über die Anrede
im Deutschen). Berlin: de Gruyter, 1963. (Quellen und
Forschungen zur Sprach- und Kulturgeschichte der germ.
Völker, Neue Folge 10).
See esp. pp. 74-87: Das Pronomen bei Chaucer.
Rev: T. Kisbye, JEGP, 62, 1963, 328-30; M. Schentke,
ZAA, 11, 1963, 303-4.

FOWLER, DAVID C. An Unusual Meaning of "Win" in Chau-
cer's Troilus and Criseyde. MLN, 69, 1954, 313-15.
"Wynne" should be translated as "complain" in T and C,
I, 390.

----------. The Date of the Cornish "Ordinalia." Med Stud,
23, 1961, 91-125.
Final -e in Chaucer.

FRENCH, W. H. General Prologue 74: Horse or Horses?
MLN, 76, 1961, 293-95.
A reply to Garland Ethel; see above. Argues that "goode"

is plural, and consequently "hors" is likewise plural.
HOMANN, ELIZABETH R. Chaucer's Use of "Gan." JEGP,
   53, 1954, 389-98.
ISAACS, NEIL D. Furlong Wey in Chaucer. NQ, 8, 1961,
   328-29.
JOHNSTON, EVERETT C. The Pronoun of Address in Chau-
   cer's Troilus. Language Quarterly (Univ of South Florida),
   1, 1962, 17-20.
KÖKERITZ, HELGE. A Guide to Chaucer's Pronunciation.
   Stockholm: Almqvist and Wiksell; New Haven, Conn.:
   Whitlock, 1954, 1961. New York: Holt, Rinehart, and
   Winston, 1962 (reprint with revised Preface).
   Rev: D. W. Robertson, QJS, 42, 1956, 326-27.
MacLEISH, ANDREW. Patterns in the Late East Midland
   Subject-Verb Cluster: A Quantitative Synchronic Descrip-
   tion. DA, 22, 865. Univ of Wisconsin, 1961.
MALONE, KEMP. Chaucer's Double Consonants and the
   Final E. Med Stud, 18, 1956, 204-7.
MANZALAOUI, M. A. Derring-do. NQ, 9, 1962, 369-70.
MURATA, YUZABURO. The Swearings in Chaucer. Studies
   in English Grammar and Linguistics: A Miscellany in Hon-
   our of Takanobu Otsuka, pp. 289-99. Tokyo: Kenkyusha,
   1958.
NATHAN, NORMAN. Pronouns of Address in the Friar's
   Tale. MLQ, 17, 1956, 39-42.
----------. Pronouns of Address in the Canterbury Tales.
   Med Stud, 21, 1959, 193-201.
NOVELLI, CORNELIUS. The Demonstrative Adjective This:
   Chaucer's Use of a Colloquial Narrative Device. Med Stud,
   19, 1957, 246-49.
PRINS, A. A. Notes on the Canterbury Tales (3). E Stud, 35,
   1954, 158-62.
   The meaning of "tregetour" in FrankT, 1141.
----------. As Fer as Last Ytaille. E Stud, 37, 1956, 111-
   16.
   The meaning of "last" in ClT, 264-66.
----------. Loke Who, What, How, When. E Stud, 43, 1962,
   165-69.
SALMON, VIVIAN. Some Connotations of "Cold" in Old and
   Middle English. MLN, 74, 1959, 314-22.

Special reference to the meaning of the proverb,
"Wommennes conseils been ful ofte colde, " NPT, 3256.
STORMS, G. A Note on Chaucer's Pronunciation of French
u. E Stud, 41, 1960, 305-8.

CANTERBURY TALES
GENERAL

See Griffith, pp. 151-63.

BALDWIN, RALPH. The Unity of the Canterbury Tales.
(Anglistica, 5.) Copenhagen: Rosenkilde og Bagger, 1955.
Portions of this monograph are reprinted in Schoeck
and Taylor, Eds., Chaucer Criticism, Vol. I, and in
Owen, Ed., Discussions of the Canterbury Tales. See
below in this section for descriptions of these collections.
Rev: Claes Schaar, SN, 28, 1956, 50-52; Ursula Brown,
RES, 8, 1957, 281-82; M.-M. Dubois, EA, 10, 1957,
147-48.

BECK, RICHARD J. Educational Expectations and Rhetorical Result in The Canterbury Tales. E Stud, 44, 1963,
241-53.

BERNDT, ROLF. Einführung in das Studium des Mittelenglischen unter Zugrundlegung des Prologs der Canterbury
Tales. Halle/Salle: Niemeyer, 1960.

BIGGAR, RAYMOND GEORGE. Langland's and Chaucer's
Treatment of Monks, Friars, and Priests. DA, 22, 1992.
Univ of Wisconsin, 1961.

CEJP, LADISLAV. O metodě Canterburských povídek.
Sborník Vysoké školy pedagogické v Olomouci, 2, 1955,
266-68.

CHUTE, MARCHETTE. On The Pleasure of Meeting Chau-
cer. EJ, 45, 1956, 373-80, 394.
DENT, A. A. Chaucer and the Horse. Leeds, 9, 1959, 1-12.
----------. Pictures from Chaucer. History Today, 10,
1960, 542-53.
Illustrated with reproductions of miniatures from Elles-
mere and of woodcuts from the Pynson (1491) ed.
----------. Fair Burgesses. History Today, 11, 1961,
753-59.
----------., and DAPHNE M. GOODALL. The Foals of
Epona. London: The Galley Press, 1962.
DUDEK, LOUIS. Art, Entertainment and Religion. QQ, 70,
1963, 413-30.
FISHER, JOHN H. Chaucer's Horses. SAQ, 60, 1961, 71-79.
HIRA, TOSHINORI. Chaucer's Gentry in the Historical Back-
ground. Essays in English and American Literature: In
Commemoration of Professor Takejiro Nakayama's Sixty-
First Birthday, pp. 325-44. Tokyo: Shohakusha, 1961.
HOWARD, DONALD R. The Conclusion of the Marriage
Group: Chaucer and the Human Condition. MP, 57, 1960,
223-32.
JORDAN, ROBERT M. Chaucer's Sense of Illusion: Roadside
Drama Reconsidered. ELH, 29, 1962, 19-33.
KNITTEL, FRANCIS ALVIN. The Women in Chaucer's Fab-
liaux. DA, 22, 3185-86. Univ of Colorado, 1961.
LINKE, HANSJÜRGEN. Szenischer Bildwechsel in Chaucers
Canterbury Tales. NS, No. 11 (Nov , 1962), pp. 485-96.
LUMIANSKY, R. M. Of Sondry Folk: The Dramatic Prin-
ciple in the Canterbury Tales. Austin: Univ of Texas
Press, 1955.
    Rev: Basil Cottle, JEGP, 55, 1956, 292-93; J. Edwin
Whitesell, Expl, March, 1956; Howard R. Patch, MLN, 71,
1956, 299-301; W. W. Lawrence, Spec, 31, 1956, 179-82;
John Lawlor, RES, 8, 1957, 181-83.
MROCZKOWSKI, PRZEMYSLAW. Mediaeval Art and Aes-
thetics in The Canterbury Tales. Spec, 33, 1958, 204-21.
OWEN, CHARLES A., JR. Chaucer's Canterbury Tales:
Aesthetic Design in Stories of the First Day. E Stud, 35,
1954, 49-56.

----------. Morality as a Comic Motif in the Canterbury Tales. CE, 16, 1955, 226-32.

----------. The Development of the Canterbury Tales. JEGP, 57, 1958, 449-76.

----------. The Earliest Plan of the Canterbury Tales. Med Stud, 21, 1959, 202-10.

----------, Ed. Discussions of the Canterbury Tales. Boston: D. C. Heath, 1962.

A collection of essays which originally appeared in journals or as portions of books; these essays are grouped under four headings: I. Early Comment and Criticism (Spenser to Arnold); II. The Prologue and Frame; III. The Tales; IV. General. For similar collections of essays, see Schoeck and Taylor (2 vols.) and Wagenknecht in section General Criticism.

RUGGIERS, PAUL G. The Form of the Canterbury Tales: Respice Fines. CE, 17, 1956, 439-43.

SAVAGE, JAMES E. The Marriage Problems in the Canterbury Tales. MissQ, 9, 1955, 27-29.

SCHOECK, RICHARD J., and JEROME TAYLOR, Eds. Chaucer Criticism. Vol. I: The Canterbury Tales. Notre Dame, Ind.: Univ of Notre Dame Press, 1960.

See section General Criticism for a description of this collection.

SELLS, ARTHUR LYTTON. Animal Poetry in French and English Literature and the Greek Tradition. Bloomington, Ind.: Indiana Univ Press, 1955. (Humanities Series, 35.)

SUDO, JUN. The Order of the Canterbury Tales Reconsidered. HSELL, 10, 1963, 77-89.

WHITE, BEATRICE. Two Chaucer Notes. 1: Proper Names in the Canterbury Tales; 2: A Minced Oath in Sir Thopas. NM, 64, 1963, 170-75.

WILLIAMS, CLEM CARY. The Genre and Art of the Old French Fabliaux: A Preface to the Study of Chaucer's Tales of the Fabliau Type. Unpub. Doct. Diss., Yale Univ, 1961.

PROLOGUE
General and Lines 1-42, 714-858

See Griffith, pp. 163-67.

ADAMS, GEORGE ROY. Chaucer's General Prologue: A
Study in Tradition and the Individual Talent. DA, 22, 2382.
Univ of Oklahoma, 1962.
BAUM, PAULL F. Canterbury Tales A24. MLN, 69, 1954,
551-52.
The meaning of "Wel nyne and twenty" pilgrims.
BROOKS, HAROLD F. Chaucer's Pilgrims: The Artistic
Order of the Portraits in the Prologue. London: Methuen;
New York: Barnes and Noble, 1962.
CUNNINGHAM, J. V. Tradition and Poetic Structure: Essays
in Literary History and Criticism. Denver, Colo.: Alan
Swallow, 1960.
See Chapter entitled Convention as Structure: The Pro-
logue to the Canterbury Tales.
DANBY, JOHN F. Eighteen Lines of Chaucer's Prologue.
CQ, 2, 1960, 28-32.
The first eighteen lines of the Prologue.
DUNLEAVY, GARETH W. Natural Law as Chaucer's Ethi-
cal Absolute. Trans. Wisconsin Academy of Sciences,
Arts, and Letters, 52, 1963, 177-87.
ENKVIST, N. E. The Seasons of the Year: Chapters on a
Motif from Beowulf to the Shepherd's Calendar. Helsing-
fors, 1957. (Societas Scientiarum Fennica. Commentati-
ones Humanarum Litterarum, 22.)
EVANS, ROBERT O. Whan That Aprill(e)? NQ, 4, 1957,
234-37.
HART, JAMES A. The Droghte of March: A Common Mis-
understanding. TSLL, 4, 1962-63, 525-29.
HOFFMAN, ARTHUR W. Chaucer's Prologue to Pilgramage:
The Two Voices. ELH, 21, 1954, 1-16.
Reprinted in Owen (Discussions) and in Wagenknecht
(Modern Essays in Criticism).
HYAMS, C. BARRY, and KARL H. REICHERT. The Month
of April in English Poetry (with Special Reference to

Geoffrey Chaucer and T. S. Eliot--A Double Lesson). NS,
Nov, 1957, 522-28.

LUMIANSKY, R. M. Benoit's Portraits and Chaucer's General Prologue. JEGP, 55, 1956, 431-38.

MAGOUN, F. P., JR. Canterbury Tales A11. MLN, 70,
1955, 399.
Argues that "Nature" in line 11 is a personification and
should thus be capitalized.

NEVO, RUTH. Chaucer: Motive and Mask in the General
Prologue. MLR, 58, 1963, 1-9.

OWEN, CHARLES A., JR. The Twenty-Nine Pilgrims and
the Three Priests. MLN, 76, 1961, 392-97.

REIDY, JOHN. Grouping of Pilgrims in the General Prologue
to the Canterbury Tales. PMASAL, 47, 1962, 595-603.
Identifies six "groups" of pilgrims.

STEADMAN, JOHN M. Chaucer's Thirty Pilgrims and
Activa Vita. Neophil, 45, 1961, 224-30.
Symbolic significance of the number thirty within the
medieval exegetical tradition.

SWART, J. The Construction of Chaucer's General Prologue. Neophil, 38, 1954, 127-36.

USSERY, HULING EAKIN, JR. Chaucer's Pilgrims: Three
Studies in the Real and the Ideal. DA, 24, 2491. Univ of
Michigan, 1963.
The "historical backgrounds of three pilgrims, Monk,
Clerk, and Physician, are studied in detail."

WOOLF, ROSEMARY. Chaucer as a Satirist in the General
Prologue to the Canterbury Tales. CQ, 1, 1959, 150-57.
See reply by Cliff Tucker in a letter to the Editors of
CQ (1, 262).

Knight, Lines 43-78
See Griffith, pp. 167-68.

ETHEL, GARLAND. Horse or Horses: A Chaucerian Textual Problem. MLN, 75, 1960, 97-101.
See W. H. French, below.

FRENCH, W. H. General Prologue 74: Horse or Horses?
MLN, 76, 1961, 293-95.
A reply to Garland Ethel, above.

NEUSE, RICHARD. The Knight: The First Mover in Chaucer's Human Comedy. UTQ, 31, 1962, 299-315.
    Considers the narrator of KnT as an extension and
completion of the portrait in GP.
SCHLAUCH, MARGARET. King Arthur in the Baltic Towns.
Bulletin Bibliographique de la Société Internationale Ar-
thurienne, No. 11, 1959, pp. 75-80.
    "A poet like Chaucer . . . would have more than one
reason for envisaging the Baltic area as an appropriate
scene for his Knight's adventurings."

Squire, Lines 79-100
See Griffith, p. 168.

GAYLORD, ALAN. A85-88: Chaucer's Squire and the Glo-
rious Campaign. PMASAL, 45, 1960, 341-60.

Yeoman, Lines 101-17
See Griffith, p. 168.

BIRNEY, EARLE. The Squire's Yeoman. REL, 1, 1960,
9-18.
    See reply by Stoddard Malarkey, below.
MALARKEY, STODDARD. Chaucer's Yeoman Again. CE,
24, 1963, 289-90, 295.
    Rejects Earle Birney's suggestion (above) that the Yeo-
man is the Squire's servant.

Prioress, Nun, and Three Priests, Lines 118-64
See Griffith, pp. 168-72.

LYNCH, JAMES J. The Prioress's Greatest Oath, Once
More. MLN, 72, 1957, 242-49.
    Identifies St. Loy as St. Eulalia rather than as St. Eli-
gius.
MANLEY, FRANCIS. Chaucer's Rosary and Donne's Brace-
let: Ambiguous Coral. MLN, 74, 1959, 385-88.
    GP, 158-62, and Donne's poem, The Token.
SCHOECK, RICHARD J. Chaucer's Prioress: Mercy and
Tender Heart. The Bridge: A Yearbook of Judaeo-Christian

Studies (New York: Pantheon Books), 2, 1956, 239-55.
Reprinted in slightly revised form in Schoeck and Tay-
lor, Eds., Chaucer Criticism, Vol. I, pp. 245-58.
STEADMAN, JOHN M. The Prioress' Dogs and Benedictine
Discipline. MP, 54, 1956, 1-6.
----------. Hir Gretteste Ooth: The Prioress, St. Eligius,
and St. Godebertha. Neophil, 43, 1959, 49-57.
----------. The Prioress' Brooch and St. Leonard. E Stud,
44, 1963, 350-53.

Monk, Lines 165-207
See Griffith, pp. 172-73.

BEICHNER, PAUL E., C. S. C. Daun Piers, Monk and
Business Administrator. Spec, 34, 1959, 611-19.
Reprinted in Schoeck and Taylor, Eds., Chaucer Criti-
cism, Vol. I, pp. 52-62.

Friar, Lines 208-69
See Griffith, pp. 173-74.

BLOOMFIELD, MORTON W. The Magic of In Principio.
MLN, 70, 1955, 559-65.
CAWLEY, A. C. Chaucer's Summoner, the Friar's Sum-
moner and the Friar's Tale. Leeds, 8, 1957, 173-80.
MUSCATINE, CHARLES. The Name of Chaucer's Friar.
MLN, 70, 1955, 169-72.
REISS, EDMUND. Chaucer's Friar and the Man in the Moon.
JEGP, 62, 1963, 481-85.
WHITESELL, J. EDWIN. Chaucer's Lisping Friar. MLN,
71, 1956, 160-61.
WILLIAMS, ARNOLD. Two Notes on Chaucer's Friars. MP,
54, 1956, 117-20.
See earlier article by Williams (Spec, 28), Griffith,
p. 209.
----------. The Limitour of Chaucer's Time and His Limi-
tacioun. SP, 57, 1960, 463-78.

Merchant, Lines 270-84
See Griffith, pp. 174-75.

STILLWELL, GARDINER. Chaucer's Merchant: No Debts?
JEGP, 57, 1958, 192-96.

Clerk, Lines 285-308
See Griffith, pp. 175-76.

LAVIN, J. A. The Clerk of Oxenford in Oral Tradition.
New York Folklore Quarterly, 17, 1961, 61-64.
MORSE, J. MITCHELL. Chaucer: A Meaning of Philosophye.
NQ, 2, 1955, 11.
----------. The Philosophy of the Clerk of Oxenford. MLQ,
19, 1958, 3-20.
Primarily concerned with ClT.
SIMMONDS, JAMES D. Hende Nicholas and the Clerk. NQ,
9, 1962, 446.

Franklin, Lines 331-60
See Griffith, pp. 176-77.

BIRNEY, EARLE. The Franklin's Sop in Wyn. NQ, 6, 1959,
345-47.

Tradesmen, Lines 361-78
See Griffith, p. 177.

GARBÁTY, THOMAS JAY. Chaucer's Guildsmen and Their
Fraternity. JEGP, 59, 1960, 691-709.
Suggests that the Tradesmen were members of a parish
guild, most likely the Guild of St. Fabian and St. Sebastian
of St. Botolph's Church in Aldersgate. See McCutchan,
below, for opposing view.
LISCA, PETER. Chaucer's Gildsmen and Their Cook. MLN,
70, 1955, 321-24.
McCUTCHAN, J. WILSON. A Solempne and a Greet Frater-
nitee. PMLA, 74, 1959, 313-17.
Suggests that the Tradesmen were members of a craft
fraternity, most likely that of the Drapers. See Garbaty,
above, for an opposing view.

Cook, Lines 379-87
See Griffith, pp. 177-78.

LISCA, PETER. Chaucer's Gildsmen and Their Cook.
MLN, 70, 1955, 321-24.

Shipman, Lines 388-410
See Griffith, p. 178.

DONOVAN, MORTIMER J. Chaucer's Shipman and the In-
tegrity of His Cargo. MLR, 50, 1955, 489-90.

Physician, Lines 411-44
See Griffith, pp. 179-80.

AIKEN, PAULINE. Vincent of Beauvais and the "Houres"
of Chaucer's Physician. SP, 53, 1956, 22-24.
GRENNEN, JOSEPH E. Double-Entendre and the Doctour
of Phisik. ANQ, 1, 1963, 131-32.

Wife of Bath, Lines 445-76
See Griffith, p. 180.

BIGGINS, D. Chaucer's General Prologue, A467. NQ, 7,
1960, 129-30.
PRATT, ROBERT A. The Development of the Wife of Bath.
Pp. 45-79 in Studies in Medieval Literature, edited by
MacEdward Leach. Philadelphia: Univ of Pennsylvania
Press; London: Oxford Univ Press, 1961.
    Professor Pratt discusses the means by which Chaucer
was able to "enlarge and develop" the "early simple por-
trait" which appears in GP.

Parson, Lines 477-528
See Griffith, pp. 180-81.

BODE, EDWARD L. The Source of Chaucer's Rusted Gold.
Med Stud, 24, 1962, 369-70.
ROCKWELL, K. A. Canterbury Tales: General Prologue,

526; The Wife of Bath's Prologue, 435: Spiced Conscience.
NQ, 4, 1957, 84.

Miller, Lines 542-66
See Griffith, pp. 181-82.

BLOCK, EDWARD A. Chaucer's Millers and Their Bag-
pipes. Spec, 29, 1954, 239-43.
JONES, GEORGE F. Chaucer and the Medieval Miller. MLQ,
16, 1955, 3-15.
MANN, H. GEORGE. Canterbury Tales, Prologue, Line
559. NQ, 1, 1954, 37.
STEADMAN, JOHN M. An Honest Miller? (Canterbury
Tales, 555). NQ, 9, 1962, 6.
WHITING, B. J. Miller's Head Revisited. MLN, 69, 1954,
309-10.

Manciple, Lines 567-86
See Griffith, p. 182.

BIRNEY, EARLE. Chaucer's Gentil Manciple and His Gentil Tale. NM, 61, 1960, 257-67.

Reeve, Lines 587-622
See Griffith, p. 182.

FOREHAND, BROOKS. Old Age and Chaucer's Reeve.
PMLA, 69, 1954, 984-89.

Summoner, Lines 623-68
See Griffith, pp. 182-83.

BIGGINS, D. More Chaucerian Ambiguities: A652, 664,
D1346. NQ, 9, 165-67.
----------. Pulling Finches and Woodcocks: A Comment.
E Stud, 44, 1963, 278.
    A comment on Ericson's note, below in this section.
CAWLEY, A. C. Chaucer's Summoner, the Friar's Sum-
moner and the Friar's Tale. Leeds, 8, 1957, 173-80.

ERICSON, ESTON EVERETT. Pulling Finches and Wood-
cocks. E Stud, 42, 1961, 306.
See comment by Biggins, above in this section.
GARBÁTY, THOMAS JAY. Chaucer's Summoner: An
Example of the Assimilation Lag in Scholarship. PMASAL,
47, 1962, 605-11.
----------. The Summoner's Occupational Disease. Medi-
cal History, 7, 1963, 348-58.
KASKE, R. E. The Summoner's Garleek, Oynons, and eek
Lekes. MLN, 74, 1959, 481-84.
MORRIS, HARRY. Some Uses of Angel Iconography in Eng-
lish Literature. CL, 10, 1958, 36-44.
Explains that the detail of the Summoner's "fyr-reed
cherubynnes face" (GP, 624) departs from the usual icon-
ography of the Middle Ages.
PACE, GEORGE B. Physiognomy and Chaucer's Summoner
and Alisoun. Traditio, 18, 1962, 417-20.

Pardoner, Lines 669-714
See Griffith, pp. 183-84.

BIGGINS, D. Chaucer's General Prologue, A163. NQ, 6,
1959, 435-36.
A reinforcement of Baum's suggestion (see section
Style) that line 673 of GP contains a pun on the word "bur-
doun"; for additional evidence, see the article by Miller,
below in this section.
----------. Chaucer's General Prologue, A696-698. NQ, 7,
1960, 93-95.
BLOOMFIELD, MORTON W. The Pardons of Pamplona and
the Pardoner of Rounceval: Piers Plowman, B XVII, 252
(C XX, 218). PQ, 35, 1956, 60-68.
ETHEL, GARLAND. Chaucer's Worste Shrewe: The Par-
doner. MLQ, 20, 1959, 211-27.
MILLER, B. D. H. Chaucer's General Prologue, A673:
Further Evidence. NQ, 7, 1960, 404-6.
See note by Biggins, above in this section.
SCHAUT, QUENTIN L. Chaucer's Pardoner and Indulgen-
ces. Greyfriar 1961, pp. 25-39.

Chaucer the Pilgrim
Not listed in Griffith.

DONALDSON, E. TALBOT. Chaucer the Pilgrim. PMLA,
   69, 1954, 928-36.
   Describes a narrative persona who is "usually, acutely
   unaware of the significance of what he sees, no matter
   how sharply he sees it." For opposing view, see John M.
   Major, below in this section. Professor Donaldson's essay
   is reprinted in Schoeck and Taylor, Eds., Chaucer Criticism, Vol. I, and in Owen, Ed., Discussions of the Canterbury Tales.
DUNCAN, EDGAR H. Narrator's Points of View in the Por-
   trait-sketches, Prologue to the Canterbury Tales. Essays
   in Honor of Walter Clyde Curry, pp. 77-101. Nashville,
   Tenn.: Vanderbilt Univ Press, 1954.
KELLOGG, A(LFRED) L. Chaucer's Self-Portrait and
   Dante's. MAE, 29, 1960, 119-20.
   An attempt to resolve the "supposed contradiction between the gregarious Chaucer of the General Prologue and
   the aloof Chaucer of Sir Thopas."
MAJOR, JOHN M. The Personality of Chaucer the Pilgrim.
   PMLA, 75, 1960, 160-62.
   A reply to Donaldson's essay, above in this section. The
   essay concludes that "to see Chaucer the pilgrim as anyone
   other than a marvelously alert, ironic, facetious master
   of every situation is to misread the Canterbury Tales."
WOOLF, ROSEMARY. Chaucer as a Satirist in the General
   Prologue to the Canterbury Tales. CQ, 1, 1959, 150-57.
   See reply by Cliff Tucker, ibid., 262. Both Woolf and
   Tucker consider the pilgrim-narrator.

THE KNIGHT'S TALE

See Griffith, pp. 184-92.

For editions and modernizations, see appropriate
sections.

ARNOTT, PETER D. The Origins of Medieval Theatre in

the Round. Theatre Notebook, 15, 1961, 84-87.

The author compares the "noble theatre" in KnT, 1885-92, with the setting of The Castle of Perseverance described in The Medieval Theater in the Round (1957) by Dr. Richard Southern.

HALVERSON, JOHN. Aspects of Order in the "Knight's Tale." SP, 57, 1960, 606-21.

KASKE, R. E. The Knight's Interruption of the Monk's Tale. ELH, 24, 1957, 249-68.

KEEN, MAURICE. Brotherhood in Arms. History, 47, 1962, 1-17.

KOVETZ, GENE H. Canterbury Tales A2349-52. NQ, 5, 1958, 236-37.

LLOYD, MICHAEL. A Defence of Arcite. EM, 10, 1959, 11-25.

A reply to William Frost, An Interpretation of Chaucer's Knight's Tale. See Griffith, p. 187.

McKENZIE, JAMES J. A Chaucerian Emendation. NQ, 1, 1954, 463.

KnT, 1454.

----------. Chaucer's The Knight's Tale, 1053. Expl, 20, 1962, Item 69.

MADDEN, WILLIAM A. "Some Philosophical Aspects of The Knight's Tale": A Reply. CE, 20, 1959, 193-94.

A reply to the article by Paul G. Ruggiers, listed below in this section.

MITCHELL, EDWARD R. The Two Mayings in Chaucer's "Knight's Tale." MLN, 71, 1956, 560-64.

NAKATANI, KIICHIRO. A Perpetual Prison: The Design of Chaucer's The Knight's Tale. HSELL, 9, 1963, 75-89.

NEUSE, RICHARD. The Knight: The First Mover in Chaucer's Human Comedy. UTQ, 31, 1962, 299-315.

PARR, JOHNSTONE. Chaucer's Cherles Rebellyng. MLN, 69, 1954, 393-94.

Glosses "cherles rebellyng" (A2459) as an astrological reference, not as a political allusion.

PRATT, ROBERT A. "Joye after Wo" in The Knight's Tale. JEGP, 57, 1958, 416-23.

QUINN, BETTY NYE. Venus, Chaucer and Peter Bersuire. Spec, 38, 1963, 479-80.

Additional evidence in support of the article by John M.
Steadman, below in this section.
ROWLAND, BERYL. Chaucer's The Knight's Tale, A1810.
Expl, 21, 1963, Item 73.
RUGGIERS, PAUL G. Some Philosophical Aspects of The
Knight's Tale. CE, 19, 1958, 296-302.
See reply, above in this section, by William A. Madden.
SALTER, ELIZABETH. Chaucer: The Knight's Tale and The
Clerk's Tale. (Studies in English Literature, edited by
David Daiches.) London: Edward Arnold, 1962; Great
Neck, N.Y.: Barron, 1963 (Barron's Educational Series).
Rev: D. S. Brewer, NQ, 10, 1963, 231-32.
SCHNYDER, HANS. Aspects of Kingship in Sir Gawain and
the Green Knight. E Stud, 40, 1959, 289-94.
Arthur is compared with Theseus, the more ideal of
the two "kings."
STEADMAN, JOHN M. Venus' Citole in Chaucer's Knight's
Tale and Berchorius. Spec, 34, 1959, 620-24.
A reply to the article by Ernest H. Wilkins, below in
this section. Steadman suggests that the detail of the
citole in Chaucer's portrait of Venus (A1955-66) is de-
rived from Berchorius' Ovidius moralizatus. Supporting
evidence provided by Betty Nye Quinn, above in this section.
THURSTON, PAUL THAYER. Artistic Ambivalence in Chaucer's Knight's Tale. Unpub. Doct. Diss., Univ of Florida,
1961.
UNDERWOOD, DALE. The First of The Canterbury Tales.
ELH, 26, 1959, 455-69.
WHITTOCK, TREVOR. Chaucer's Knight's Tale. Theoria,
13, 1958, 27-38.
WILKINS, ERNEST H. Descriptions of Pagan Divinities
from Petrarch to Chaucer. Spec, 32, 1957, 511-22.
Suggests that the descriptions of Venus, Mars, and
Mercury in KnT derive ultimately from Petrarch's Africa,
and that the immediate source is the Libellus de deorum
imaginibus ascribed to "Albricus Philosophus." See
John M. Steadman's reply, above in this section.
WORDSWORTH, JONATHAN. A Link Between the Knight's
Tale and the Miller's. MAE, 27, 1958, 21.

THE MILLER'S TALE

See Griffith, pp. 192-95.

BEICHNER, PAUL E. Characterization in the Miller's Tale.
Pp. 117-29 in Chaucer Criticism, edited by Richard J.
Schoeck and Jerome Taylor, Vol. I: The Canterbury Tales.
Notre Dame, Ind.: Univ of Notre Dame Press, 1960.
See section General Criticism for full description of
this volume.
BIRNEY, EARLE. The Inhibited and the Uninhibited: Ironic
Structure in the "Miller's Tale." Neophil, 44, 1960, 333-
38.
BOLTON, W. F. The Miller's Tale: An Interpretation. Med
Stud, 24, 1962, 83-94.
BOOTHMAN, JANET. "Who Hath No Wyf, He is No Coke-
wold": A Study of John and January in Chaucer's Miller's
and Merchant's Tales. Thoth, 4, 1963, 3-14.
CLINE, RUTH H. Three Notes on The Miller's Tale. HLQ,
26, 1963, 131-45.
DONALDSON, E. TALBOT. Chaucer's Miller's Tale,
A3483-86. MLN, 69, 1954, 310-13.
----------. Idiom of Popular Poetry in the Miller's Tale.
Pp. 27-51 in Explication as Criticism: Selected Papers
from the English Institute 1941-1952, edited by W. K.
Wimsatt, Jr. Columbia Univ Press, 1963.
Reprinted from Eng Inst Essays, 1949-1950, edited by
Alan S. Downer, pp. 116-40. See Griffith, pp. 193-94.
HARDER, KELSIE B. Chaucer's Use of the Mystery Plays
in the Miller's Tale. MLQ, 17, 1956, 193-98.
KASKE, R. E. The Canticum Canticorum in the Miller's
Tale. SP, 59, 1962, 479-500.
KREUZER, JAMES R. The Swallow in Chaucer's Miller's
Tale. MLN, 73, 1958, 81.
O'CONNOR, JOHN J. The Astrological Background of the
Miller's Tale. Spec, 31, 1956, 120-25.
OLSON, PAUL A. Poetic Justice in the Miller's Tale. MLQ,
24, 1963, 227-36.
PACE, GEORGE B. Physiognomy and Chaucer's Summoner
and Alisoun. Traditio, 18, 1962, 417-20.

REED, MARY BROOKBANK. Chaucer's Sely Carpenter.
    PQ, 41, 1962, 768-69.
SIEGEL, PAUL N. Comic Irony in The Miller's Tale. BUSE,
    4, 1960, 114-20.
SIMMONDS, JAMES D. "Hende Nicholas" and the Clerk.
    NQ, 9, 1962, 446.
STILLWELL, GARDINER. The Language of Love in Chau-
    cer's Miller's and Reeve's Tales and in the Old French
    Fabliaux. JEGP, 54, 1955, 693-99.
WORDSWORTH, JONATHAN. A Link Between the Knight's
    Tale and the Miller's. MAE, 27, 1958, 21.

THE REEVE'S PROLOGUE AND TALE

See Griffith, pp. 195-97.

BLOCK, EDWARD A. Chaucer's Millers and Their Bag-
    pipes. Spec, 29, 1954, 239-43.
-----------. ". . . And It Is Half-Wey Pryme." Spec, 32,
    1957, 826-33.
COPLAND, M. The Reeve's Tale: Harlotrie or Sermonyng?
    MAE, 31, 1962, 14-32.
ELIASON, NORMAN E. Some Word-Play in Chaucer's
    Reeve's Tale. MLN, 71, 1956, 162-64.
EMERSON, KATHERINE T. The Question of "Lusty Malyne."
    NQ, 4, 1957, 277-78.
FOREHAND, BROOKS. Old Age and Chaucer's Reeve.
    PMLA, 69, 1954, 984-89.
HINTON, NORMAN D. Two Names in The Reeve's Tale.
    Names, 9, 1961, 117-20.
JONES, GEORGE F. Chaucer and the Medieval Miller.
    MLQ, 16, 1955, 3-15.
KASKE, R. E. An Aube in the "Reeve's Tale." ELH, 26,
    1959, 295-310.
MacLAINE, A. H. Chaucer's Wine-Cask Image: Word Play
    in the Reeve's Prologue. MAE, 31, 1962, 129-31.
OLSON, PAUL A. The Reeve's Tale: Chaucer's Measure
    for Measure. SP, 59, 1962, 1-17.
PRATT, ROBERT A. Chaucer and the Holy Cross of Brom-
    holm. MLN, 70, 1955, 324-25.

----------. Symkyn Koude "Turne Coppes": The Reeve's
   Tale 3928. JEGP, 59, 1960, 208-11.
STEADMAN, JOHN M. Simkin's Camus Nose: A Latin Pun
   in the Reeve's Tale? MLN, 75, 1960, 4-8.
STILLWELL, GARDINER. The Language of Love in Chau-
   cer's Miller's and Reeve's Tales and in the Old French
   Fabliaux. JEGP, 54, 1955, 693-99.
TURNER, W. ARTHUR. Chaucer's "Lusty Malyne." NQ,
   1, 1954, 232-33.

THE COOK'S PROLOGUE AND TALE

See Griffith, pp. 197-98.

EMERSON, KATHERINE T. Chaucer's Canterbury Tales,
   A4353. Expl, 16, 1958, Item 51.
   Identification of the Cook with "Roger Knyght de Ware,
   Cook."
LUMIANSKY, R. M. Chaucer's Cook-Host Relationship.
   Med Stud, 17, 1955, 208-9.

INTRODUCTION, PROLOGUE,
AND THE MAN OF LAW'S TALE

See Griffith, pp. 198-201.

BOWEN, ROBERT O. Chaucer, The Man of Law's Introduction and Tale. MLN, 71, 1956, 165.
BURROW, J. "A maner Latyn corrupt." MAE, 30, 1961,
   33-37.
DEAN, RUTH J. The Manuscripts of Nicholas Trevet's
   Anglo-Norman Chronicles. M and H, Fasc. 14, 1962,
   pp. 95-105.
FOWLER, DAVID C. An Accused Queen in "The Lass of
   Roch Royal" (Child 76). Journal of American Folk-Lore,
   71, 1958, 553-63.
   A study of the Constance story in a variety of forms,
   including Chaucer's version ("more typical of romance as
   opposed to folklore") of the story.

ISAACS, NEIL D. Constance in Fourteenth-Century Eng-
land. NM, 59, 1958, 260-77.
----------. The Man of Law's Merchant-Source. ANQ, 1,
1962, 52-53.
JONES, CLAUDE E. Chaucer's Custance. NM, 64, 1963,
175-80.
SEVERS, J. BURKE. A Lost Chaucerian Stanza? MLN, 74,
1959, 193-98.
YUNCK, JOHN A. Religious Elements in Chaucer's "Man of
Law's Tale." ELH, 27, 1960, 249-61.

THE WIFE OF BATH'S PROLOGUE AND TALE

See Griffith, pp. 202-6.

ACKERMAN, ROBERT W. English Rimed and Prose Roman-
ces. Chapter xxxvii (pp. 480-519) in Arthurian Literature
in The Middle Ages: A Collaborative History, edited by
Roger Sherman Loomis. Oxford: Clarendon Press, 1959.
Discussion of WBT: pp. 501-5.
ALBRECHT, W. P. A Seventeenth-Century Text of Thomas
of Erceldoune. MAE, 23, 1954, 88-95.
Analogue of WBT.
----------. The Loathly Lady in "Thomas of Erceldoune"
with a Text of the Poem Printed in 1652. Albuquerque,
N.M.: Univ of New Mexico Press, 1954. (Univ of New
Mexico Publications in Language and Literature, 11.)
BAKER, DONALD C. Chaucer's Clerk and the Wife of Bath
on the Subject of Gentilesse. SP, 59, 1962, 631-40.
BOYD, BEVERLY. The Wife of Bath's Gay Lente. ANQ, 1,
1963, 85-86.
BRADLEY, SISTER RITAMARY, C. H. M. "The Wife of
Bath's Tale" and the Mirror Tradition. JEGP, 55, 1956,
624-30.
CHRISTIE, SISTER MARY JOANNES. The Provenance of
Chaucer's Self Portraits: the Pardoner and the Wife of
Bath. Fordham Univ Diss., 1958.
EISNER, SIGMUND. A Tale of Wonder: a Source Study of
The Wife of Bath's Tale. DA, 15, 1062. Columbia Univ,
1955.

----------. A Tale of Wonder: A Source Study of the Wife
    of Bath's Tale. Wexford, Ireland: John English and Co.,
    1957.
    Rev: Robert T. Meyer, MLN, 74, 1959, 734-35; Guy
    Bourquin, EA, 12, 1959, 61; John MacQueen, RES, 10,
    1959, 406-7; Margaret Schlauch, MAE, 28, 1959, 131-33;
    Bernard F. Huppé, MLQ, 20, 1960, 97-98; Robert W.
    Ackermann, Ang, 78, 1961, 85-87; Charles W. Dunn,
    Spec, 36, 1961, 480-82.
HALLER, ROBERT SPENCER. The Old Whore in Mediae-
    val Thought: Variations on a Convention. DA, 22, 564-65.
    Princeton Univ, 1960.
HOFFMAN, RICHARD L. The Wife of Bath and the Dunmow
    Bacon. NQ, 10, 1963, 9-11.
LUMIANSKY, R. M. Aspects of the Relationship of Boc-
    caccio's Il Filostrato with Benoît's Roman de Troie and
    Chaucer's Wife of Bath's Tale. Italica, 31, 1954, 1-7.
MALONE, KEMP. The Wife of Bath's Tale. MLR, 57, 1962,
    481-91.
MARGULIES, CECILE STOLLER. The Marriages and the
    Wealth of the Wife of Bath. Med Stud, 24, 1962, 210-16.
MROCZKOWSKI, PRZEMYSLAW. Incubi and Friars. KN,
    8, 1961, 191-92.
PRATT, ROBERT A. Chaucer and Isidore on Why Men Mar-
    ry. MLN, 74, 1959, 293-94.
----------. The Development of the Wife of Bath. Pp. 45-
    79 in Studies in Medieval Literature, edited by MacEd-
    ward Leach. Philadelphia: Univ of Pennsvlvania Press;
    London: Oxford Univ Press, 1961.
----------. Jankyn's Book of Wikked Wyves: Medieval
    Antimatrimonial Propaganda in the Universities. AnM,
    3, 1962, 5-27.
----------. Chaucer's "natal Jove" and "Seint Jerome . . .
    agayn Jovinian." JEGP, 61, 1962, 244-48.
----------. Saint Jerome in Jankyn's Book of Wikked Wyves.
    Crit, 5, 1963, 316-22.
ROCKWELL, K. A. Canterbury Tales: General Prologue,
    526; The Wife of Bath's Prologue, 435: "Spiced Con-
    science." NQ, 4, 1957, 84.
SALTER, F. M. The Tragic Figure of the Wyf of Bath.

Proc and Trans Royal Soc of Canada, 3rd ser., 48, 1954,
Sect. 2, 1-14.
SILVERSTEIN, THEODORE. Wife of Bath and the Rhetoric
of Enchantment; or, How to Make a Hero See in the Dark.
MP, 58, 1961, 153-73.
STEADMAN, JOHN M. The Book-Burning Episode in the
Wife of Bath's Prologue: Some Additional Analogues.
PMLA, 74, 1959, 521-25.
TOWNSEND, FRANCIS G. Chaucer's Nameless Knight.
MLR, 49, 1954, 1-4.
WHITTOCK, TREVOR. The Marriage Debate. I. Theoria,
No. 14, 1960, 55-66.
WILKS, MICHAEL. Chaucer and the Mystical Marriage in
Medieval Political Thought. BJRL, 44, 1962, 489-530.

THE FRIAR'S PROLOGUE AND TALE

See Griffith, pp. 207-8.

BAKER, DONALD C. Exemplary Figures as Characteri-
zing Devices in the Friar's Tale and the Summoner's
Tale. UMSE, 3, 1962, 35-41.
BEICHNER, PAUL E. Baiting the Summoner. MLQ, 22,
1961, 367-76.
BIGGINS, D(ENNIS). More Chaucerian Ambiguities: A652,
664, D1346. NQ, 9, 1962, 165-67.
BIRNEY, EARLE. After His Ymage--The Central Ironies
of the Friar's Tale. Med Stud, 21, 1959, 17-35.
BONJOUR, ADRIEN. Aspects of Chaucer's Irony in The
Friar's Tale. EC, 11, 1961, 121-27.
CAWLEY, A. C. Chaucer's Summoner, the Friar's Sum-
moner and the Friar's Tale. Leeds, 8, 1957, 173-80.
HARRISON, THOMAS P. Chaucer's "Wariangles." NQ, 1,
1954, 189.
    FriarT, 1407-8.
HIEATT, CONSTANCE. Oaths in the Friar's Tale. NQ, 7,
1960, 5-6.
KELLOGG, A(LFRED) L. Chaucer's Friar's Tale: Line
1314. NQ, 6, 1959, 190-92.

MROCZKOWSKI, PRZEMYSLAW. The Friar's Tale and Its
    Pulpit Background. English Studies Today, pp. 107-20.
    2nd Ser., edited by G. A. Bonnard. Berne: Francke Ver-
    lag, 1961.
    In this volume are printed the Lectures and Papers
    read at the Fourth Conference of the International Asso-
    ciation of University Professors of English held at Lau-
    sanne and Berne, August 1959. Rev: TLS, July 14, 1961,
    434.
----------. Chaucer's Green Yeoman and Le Roman de
    Renart. NQ, 9, 1962, 325-26.
NATHAN, NORMAN. Pronouns of Address in the Friar's
    Tale. MLQ, 17, 1956, 39-42.
RICHARDSON, JANETTE. An Ambiguous Reference in
    Chaucer's Friar's Tale. Archiv, 198, 1961, 388-90.
----------. Hunter and Prey: Functional Imagery in Chau-
    cer's Friar's Tale. EM, 12, 1961, 9-20.
ROBERTSON, D. W., JR. Why the Devil Wears Green.
    MLN, 69, 1954, 470-72.
ROWLAND, BERYL. Wood . . . as an Hare (The Friar's
    Tale, 1327). NQ, 10, 1963, 168-69.

THE SUMMONER'S PROLOGUE AND TALE

See Griffith, pp. 208-9.

ADAMS, JOHN F. The Structure of Irony in The Summoner's
    Tale. EC, 12, 1962, 126-32.
BAKER, DONALD C. Witchcraft in the Dispute Between
    Chaucer's Friar and Summoner. The South Central Bul-
    letin (Tulsa, Okla.), 21, 1961, 33-36.
----------. Exemplary Figures as Characterizing Devices
    in the Friar's Tale and the Summoner's Tale. UMSE, 3,
    1962, 35-41.
BEICHNER, PAUL E. Non Alleluia Ructare. Med Stud, 18,
    1956, 135-44.
    A gloss on SumT, 1934.
BIRNEY, EARLE. Structural Irony Within the Summoner's
    Tale. Ang, 78, 1960, 204-18.

KOCH, ROBERT A. Elijah the Prophet, Founder of the Carmelite Order. Spec, 34, 1959, 547-60.
    SumT, 2116-18.
MERRILL, THOMAS F. Wrath and Rhetoric in The Summoner's Tale. TSLL, 4, 1962, 341-50.
SHAIN, CHARLES E. Pulpit Rhetoric in Three Canterbury Tales. MLN, 70, 1955, 235-45.

THE CLERK'S PROLOGUE, TALE, ENVOY AND WORDS OF THE HOST

See Griffith, pp. 209-13.

BAKER, DONALD C. Chaucer's Clerk and the Wife of Bath on the Subject of Gentilesse. SP, 59, 1962, 631-40.
BOWEN, ROBERT O. Chaucer, The Clerk's Prologue. MLN, 71, 1956, 165.
CRAIG, BARBARA M., Ed. L'Estoire de Griséldis. Lawrence, Kansas: Univ of Kansas Press, 1954. (Univ of Kansas Publications, Humanistic Studies, 31.)
HENINGER, S. K., JR. The Concept of Order in Chaucer's Clerk's Tale. JEGP, 56, 1957, 382-95.
JEFFREY, LLOYD N. Chaucer's Walter: A Study in Emotional Immaturity. Journal of Humanistic Psychology, 3, 1963, 112-19.
LANDRUM, GRAHAM G. An Interpretation of the Clerk's Tale according to Mediaeval Literary Theory, Based on a Study of Sources and Analogues. DA, 14, 1725. Princeton Univ, 1954.
MORSE, J. MITCHELL. The Philosophy of the Clerk of Oxenford. MLQ, 19, 1958, 3-20.
PRINS, A. A. As fer as last Ytaille. E Stud, 37, 1956, 111-16.
    Meaning of "last" in ClT, 264-66.
REIMAN, DONALD H. The Real Clerk's Tale; or Patient Griselda Exposed. TSLL, 5, 1963, 356-73.
ROQUES, MARIO, Ed. L'Estoire de Griséldis, en Rimes et par Personnages (1395). Publiée d'après le Manuscrit unique de la Bibliothèque Nationale. Genève: Droz; Paris:

Minard, 1957. (Textes Littéraires Français, 74.)
SALTER, ELIZABETH. Chaucer: The Knight's Tale and
   The Clerk's Tale. Studies in English Literature, edited by
   David Daiches. London: Edward Arnold, 1962; Great Neck,
   N. Y.: Barron, 1963 (Barron's Educational Series).
      Rev: D. S. Brewer, NQ, 10, 1963, 231-32.
SEVERS, J. BURKE. Did Chaucer Rearrange the Clerk's
   Envoy? MLN, 69, 1954, 472-78.

THE MERCHANT'S PROLOGUE, TALE, AND EPILOGUE

See Griffith, pp. 213-16.

BASSAN, MAURICE. Chaucer's "Cursed Monk," Constanti-
   nus Africanus. Med Stud, 24, 1962, 127-40.
      MerT, 1810-11.
BOOTHMAN, JANET. "Who Hath No Wyf, He is No Coke-
   wold": A Study of John and January in Chaucer's Miller's
   and Merchant's Tales. Thoth, 4, 1963, 3-14.
BRONSON, BERTRAND H. Afterthoughts on The Merchant's
   Tale. SP, 58, 1961, 583-96.
BURROW, J. A. Irony in the Merchant's Tale. Ang, 75,
   1957, 199-208.
DONOVAN, MORTIMER J. The Image of Pluto and Proser-
   pine in The Merchant's Tale. PQ, 36, 1957, 49-60.
GRIFFITH, PHILIP MAHONE. Chaucer's Merchant's Tale.
   Expl, 16, 1957, Item 13.
      Additional support for the pun on "lechour" in MerT,
   2257; see article by William W. Main, below in this sec-
   tion.
JORDAN, ROBERT M. The Non-Dramatic Disunity of the
   Merchant's Tale. PMLA, 78, 1963, 293-99.
KASKE, R. E. January's "Aube." MLN, 75, 1960, 1-4.
KEE, KENNETH. Two Chaucerian Gardens. Med Stud, 23,
   1961, 154-62.
      The gardens in MerT and in FrankT.
KELLOGG, A(LFRED) L. Susannah and the Merchant's
   Tale. Spec, 35, 1960, 275-79.

MAIN, WILLIAM W. Chaucer's The Merchant's Tale, 2257-
61. Expl, 14, 1955, Item 13.
   Suggests pun upon lechour in MerT, 2257; see Griffith,
above in this section, for additional evidence.
MATTHEWS, WILLIAM. Eustache Deschamps and Chaucer's
Merchant's Tale. MLR, 51, 1956, 217-20.
OLSON, PAUL A. Chaucer's Merchant and January's
"Hevene in erthe heere." ELH, 28, 1961, 203-14.
----------. The Merchant's Lombard Knight. TSLL, 3,
1961, 259-63.
SCHAAR, CLAES. The Merchànt's Tale, Amadas et Ydoine,
and Guillaume au Faucon. Bulletin de la Société Royale
des Lettres de Lund, 2, 1952-53, 87-95.
   Rev: Mia I. Gerhardt, Museum, 60, 1955, 251.
SHAIN, CHARLES E. Pulpit Rhetoric in Three Canterbury
Tales. MLN, 70, 1955, 235-45.

THE SQUIRE'S PROLOGUE AND TALE

See Griffith, pp. 216-19.

EMERSON, FRANCIS WILLARD. Cambalus in The Squire's
Tale. NQ, 5, 1958, 461.
OSGERBY, J. R. Chaucer's Squire's Tale. Use of English
(London), 11, 1959, 102-7.

THE WORDS OF THE FRANKLIN,
THE FRANKLIN'S PROLOGUE AND TALE

See Griffith, pp. 219-21.

BAKER, DONALD C. A Crux in Chaucer's Franklin's Tale:
Dorigen's Complaint. JEGP, 60, 1961, 56-64.
BENJAMIN, EDWIN B. The Concept of Order in the Frank-
lin's Tale. PQ, 38, 1959, 119-24.
DONOVAN, MORTIMER J. The Anticlaudian and Three Pas-
sages in the Franklin's Tale. JEGP, 56, 1957, 52-59.
KEE, KENNETH. Two Chaucerian Gardens. Med Stud, 23,
1961, 154-62.
LOOMIS, LAURA HIBBARD. Secular Dramatics in the

Royal Palace, Paris, 1378, 1389, and Chaucer's "Tregetoures. " Spec, 33, 1958, 242-55.
    The "tregetoures" of FrankT, 1141, are "actors, crafts-
men, artisans mécaniques"; for a different view, see
A. A. Prins (below in this section). The Loomis essay is
reprinted in Adventures in the Middle Ages: A Memorial
Collection of Essays and Studies, by Laura Hibbard
Loomis. New York: Burt Franklin, 1962.
MAGOUN, F. P. , JR. Canterbury Tales, F1541-44. MLN,
70, 1955, 173.
    Suggests that these four lines be assigned to the Frank-
lin rather than to Aurelius.
MALLIKARJUNAN, S. On Three Interpretations of Chaucer's
The Franklin's Tale. Indian Journal of English Studies,
3, 1962, 1-11.
PRINS, A. A. Notes on the Canterbury Tales (3). E Stud,
35, 1954, 158-62.
    Contends that a "tregetour" is "a magician who causes
illusions. " For a different view, see Laura Hibbard
Loomis, above in this section.

THE PHYSICIAN'S TALE

See Griffith, p. 222.

OWEN, CHARLES A. , JR. Relationship Between the Physician's Tale and the Parson's Tale. MLN, 71, 1956,
84-87.

WORDS OF THE HOST
(OR INTRODUCTION TO THE PARDONER'S TALE),
THE PARDONER'S PROLOGUE AND TALE

See Griffith, pp. 222-25.

BEICHNER, PAUL E. Chaucer's Pardoner as Entertainer.
Med Stud, 25, 1963, 160-72.
CANDELARIA, FREDERICK H. Chaucer's "Fowle Ok" and

The Pardoner's Tale. MLN, 71, 1956, 321-22.

CHRISTIE, SISTER MARY JOANNES. The Provenance of Chaucer's Self Portraits: the Pardoner and the Wife of Bath. Fordham Univ Diss., 1958.

DUINO, RUSSELL. The Tortured Pardoner. EJ, 46, 1957, 320-25.

ETHEL, GARLAND. Chaucer's Worste Shrewe: The Pardoner. MLQ, 20, 1959, 211-27.

EVANOFF, ALEXANDER. The Pardoner as Huckster: A Dissent from Kittredge. Brigham Young University Studies, 4, 1962, 209-17.

FRIEND, ALBERT C. The Dangerous Theme of the Pardoner. MLQ, 18, 1957, 305-8.

HAMP, ERIC P. St. Ninian/Ronyan Again. Celtica, 3, 1956, 290-94.

KANTOR, BETTY. The Sin of Pride in The Pardoner's Tale. Stanford Honors Essays in Humanities, 5 and 6, 1962.

McNAMARA, LEO F. The Astonishing Performance of Chaucer's Pardoner. PMASAL, 46, 1961, 597-604.

MILLER, ROBERT P. Chaucer's Pardoner, the Scriptural Eunuch, and The Pardoner's Tale. Spec, 30, 1955, 180-99.

PRATT, ROBERT A. Chaucer's Pardoner's Prologue, 444-47. Expl, 21, 1962, Item 14.

SEVERS, J. BURKE. Author's Revision in Block C of the Canterbury Tales. Spec, 29, 1954, 512-30.

SHAIN, CHARLES E. Pulpit Rhetoric in Three Canterbury Tales. MLN, 70, 1955, 235-45.

SPEIRS, JOHN. The Pardoneres Prologue and Tale. Pp. 109-17 in The Age of Chaucer, edited by Boris Ford. London, Baltimore: Penguin Books, 1954.

For a description of this volume, see under the name of the editor in section General Criticism. The Speirs essay is reprinted, in slightly revised form, from the author's Chaucer, the Maker (1951).

STEADMAN, JOHN M. "My Modres Gate" and "El Palo del Viejo." NQ, 5, 1958, 323.

STOCKTON, ERIC W. The Deadliest Sin in The Pardoner's
   Tale. TSL, 6, 1961, 47-59.
STRANG, BARBARA M. H. Who is the Old Man in The Par-
   doner's Tale? NQ, 7, 1960, 207-8.

THE SHIPMAN'S PROLOGUE OR THE EPILOGUE
OF THE MAN OF LAW's TALE (II[B^1] 1163-1190)
AND THE SHIPMAN'S TALE

See Griffith, pp. 225-26.

APPLEMAN, PHILIP. The Shipman's Tale and the Wife of
   Bath. NQ, 3, 1956, 372-73.
      A reply to Robert L. Chapman, below in this section.
CHAPMAN, ROBERT L. The Shipman's Tale Was Meant
   for the Shipman. MLN, 71, 1956, 4-5.
      See replies by Philip Appleman and William W. Law-
   rence, elsewhere in this section.
LAWRENCE, WILLIAM W. The Wife of Bath and the Ship-
   man. MLN, 72, 1957, 87-88.
      A reply to Robert L. Chapman, above in this section.
----------. Chaucer's Shipman's Tale. Spec, 33, 1958,
   56-68.
      The tale was originally written by Chaucer with the
   Wife of Bath in mind as narrator.
SINGER, ARMAND E. Bibliography of the Don Juan Theme:
   Versions and Criticism. West Virginia University Bulle-
   tin, Philological Papers (Ser. 54, Nos. 10-11), 1954.
      See the following supplements for additional references:
   Supplement to a Bibliography of the Don Juan Theme,
   WVUB, 10, 1956, 1-36; 2nd Supplement to a Bibliography
   of the Don Juan Theme: Versions and Criticism. WVUB,
   11 (Ser. 58, Nos. 11-12), 1958, 42-64.
SULLIVAN, HELEN. A Chaucerian Puzzle. A Chaucerian
   Puzzle and Other Medieval Essays, edited by N. G. Law-
   rence and J. A. Reynolds, pp. 1-46. Coral Gables,
   Florida: Univ of Miami Press, 1961.
      The author doubts that Chaucer first assigned the tale
   to the Wife of Bath.

THE PRIORESS' HEADLINK, PROLOGUE, AND TALE

See Griffith, pp. 226-28.

ANON. The Legend of Little Hugh. Western Folklore, 19,
    1960, 61-62.
BEICHNER, PAUL E., C. S. C. The Grain of Paradise.
    Spec, 36, 1961, 302-7.
BOYD, BEVERLY. The Little Clergeon's "Alma Redemp-
    toris Mater." NQ, 4, 1957, 277.
----------. Young Hugh of Lincoln and Chaucer's The Pri-
    oress's Tale. Radford Review, 14, 1960, 1-5.
BRATCHER, JAMES T. The Greyn in The Prioress's Tale.
    NQ, 10, 1963, 444-45.
COHEN, MAURICE. Chaucer's Prioress and Her Tale. A
    Study of Anal Character and Anti-Semitism. The Psycho-
    analytic Quarterly, 31, 1962, 232-49.
GAYLORD, ALAN T. The Unconquered Tale of the Prioress.
    PMASAL, 47, 1962, 613-36.
LOOMIS, ROGER SHERMAN. Was There a Play on the Mar-
    tyrdom of Hugh of Lincoln? MLN, 69, 1954, 31-34.
    Points out the error which led Manly to believe that a
    play about Hugh's martyrdom once existed. See the note
    by Leo Spitzer (below in this section), who questions
    Loomis' translation of "ludendo composuit."
MAGOUN, FRANCIS P., JR. Canterbury Tales, B1761-63,
    1839. MLN, 71, 1956, 165-66.
PRESTON, RAYMOND. Chaucer, His Prioress, the Jews,
    and Professor Robinson. NQ, 8, 1961, 7-8.
SAITZ, ROBERT L. Hugh of Lincoln and the Jews. Chicago
    Jewish Forum, 18, 1960, 308-11.
SCHOECK, RICHARD J. Chaucer's Prioress: Mercy and
    Tender Heart. The Bridge: A Yearbook of Judaeo-Chris-
    tian Studies (New York: Pantheon Books), 2, 1956, 239-55.
    Reprinted in slightly revised form in Schoeck and Tay-
    lor, Eds., Chaucer Criticism, Vol. I, pp. 245-58.
SPITZER, LEO. (Letter to the Editors), MLN, 69, 1954,
    383-84.
    Questions Loomis' translation of the Latin phrase "is-
    tos ympnos ludendo composuit" quoted in the article cited

above. Suggests that "ludendo composuit means probably
nothing more than 'he composed as a poetic exercise.'"
STEADMAN, JOHN M. The Prioress's Tale and "Granella"
of "Paradiso." Med Stud, 24, 1962, 388-91.
WENK, J. C. On the Sources of the Prioress's Tale. Med
Stud, 17, 1955, 214-19.
YUNCK, JOHN A. "Lucre of Vileynye": Chaucer's Prioress
and the Canonists. NQ, 7, 1960, 165-67.

SIR THOPAS: PROLOGUE AND TALE

See Griffith, pp. 228-31.

BLISS, A. J. Thomas Chestre: A Speculation. Litera: Stu-
dies in Lang and Lit (Univ of Istanbul), 5, 1958, 1-6.
   Chestre's Sir Launfal and Chaucer's Sir Thopas.
DONOVAN, MORTIMER J. Sir Thopas, 772-774. NM, 57,
1956, 237-46.
GREEN, A. WIGFALL. Chaucer's Sir Thopas: Meter,
Rhyme, and Contrast. UMSE, 1, 1960, 1-11.
KELLOGG, A(LFRED) L. Chaucer's Self-Portrait and Dan-
te's. MAE, 29, 1960, 119-20.
   An attempt to resolve the "supposed contradiction be-
tween the gregarious Chaucer of the General Prologue and
the aloof Chaucer of Sir Thopas."
McCRACKEN, SAMUEL. Chaucer's Sir Thopas, B^2, 1914-
1915. Expl, 17, 1959, Item 57.
   Suggests a pun on "doghty" in Sir Thopas, 724: Sire Tho-
pas wax a doghty swayn.
MELTON, JOHN L. Sir Thopas' "Charbocle." PQ, 35,
1956, 215-17.
MOORE, ARTHUR K. Sir Thopas as Criticism of Fourteenth-
Century Minstrelsy. JEGP, 53, 1954, 532-45.
ROWLAND, BERYL. "Bihold the Murye Words of the Hoost
to Chaucer." NM, 64, 1963, 48-52.
TUCKER, S. I. Sir Thopas and the Wild Beasts. RES, 10,
1959, 54-56.
WHITE, BEATRICE. Two Chaucer Notes. 1. Proper Names
in the Canterbury Tales; 2: A "Minced" Oath in Sir Thopas. NM, 64, 1963, 170-75.

MELIBEUS: HEADLINK AND TALE

See Griffith, pp. 231-32.

BRERETON, GEORGINE E. Viper into Weasel (A Note on a
Line in Chaucer's Melibee). MAE, 27, 1958, 173-74.
HARTUNG, ALBERT EDWARD. A Study of the Textual Affiliations of Chaucer's Melibeus Considered in Its Relation to the French Source. DA, 17, 2259-60. Lehigh Univ,
1957.

THE MONK'S PROLOGUE AND TALE

See Griffith, pp. 232-35.

KASKE, R. E. The Knight's Interruption of the Monk's Tale.
ELH, 24, 1957, 249-68.
LÜDEKE, HENRY. Chaucers persische Zenobia. Pp. 98-
99 in Festschrift zum 75. Geburtstag von Theodor Spira,
edited by Helmut Viebrock and Willi Erzgraber. Heidel-
berg: Carl Winter, 1961.
McDERMOTT, WILLIAM C. Chaucer and Virgil. Classica
et Mediaevalia, 23, 1962, 216-17.
  The "firy" serpent of MonT, 2105, results from a faul-
ty reading of Virgil Aeneid VI. 288.
PACE, GEORGE B. Adam's Hell. PMLA, 78, 1963, 25-35.
PRATT, ROBERT A. Chaucer and the Pillars of Hercules.
Pp. 118-25 in Studies in Honor of Ullman, edited by Lilli-
an B. Lawler and others. St. Louis, Mo.: The Classical
Bulletin, 1960.
  Refers to MonT, 2117-18.

THE NUN'S PRIEST'S PROLOGUE, TALE,
AND EPILOGUE

See Griffith, pp. 235-38.

BOSSUAT, R. Le Roman de Renard. Paris: Hatier-Boivin,
1957.
  References to NPT.

BROES, ARTHUR T. Chaucer's Disgruntled Cleric: The Nun's Priest's Tale. PMLA, 78, 1963, 156-62.

BROSNAHAN, LEGER. Does the Nun's Priest's Epilogue Contain a Link? SP, 58, 1961, 468-82.

DAHLBERG, CHARLES R. Chaucer's Cock and the Fox. JEGP, 53, 1954, 277-90.

FISH, STANLEY E. The Nun's Priest's Tale and Its Analogues. CLAJ, 5, 1962, 223-28.

GIBBONS, ROBERT F. Does the Nun's Priest's Epilogue Contain a Link? SP, 51, 1954, 21-33.

GRENNEN, JOSEPH E. Chauntecleer's "Venymous" Cathartics. NQ, 10, 1963, 286-87.

HAMM, VICTOR M. Chaucer's "Heigh Ymaginacioun." MLN, 69, 1954, 394-95.
NPT, 3217.

HITT, RALPH E. Chauntecleer as Mock-Hero of the Nun's Priest's Tale. MissQ, 12, 1959, 75-85.

HOLBROOK, DAVID. The Nonne Preestes Tale. Pp. 118-28 in The Age of Chaucer, edited by Boris Ford.
For a description of this volume, see under the name of the editor in section General Criticism.

LENAGHAN, R. T. The Nun's Priest's Fable. PMLA, 78, 1963, 300-7.

MANNING, STEPHEN. The Nun's Priest's Morality and the Medieval Attitude Toward Fables. JEGP, 59, 1960, 403-16.

MAVEETY, STANLEY R. An Approach to the Nun's Priest's Tale. CLAJ, 4, 1960, 132-37.

PAFFARD, M. K. Pertelote's Prescription. NQ, 4, 1957, 370.

STANDOP, EWALD. Zur allegorischen Deutung der Nonnes Preestes Tale. Pp. 88-97 in Festschrift zum 75. Geburtstag von Theodor Spira, edited by Helmut Viebrock and Willi Erzgraber. Heidelberg: Carl Winter, 1961.

STEADMAN, JOHN M. Chauntecleer and Medieval Natural History. Isis, 50, 1959, 236-44.

----------. Flattery and the Moralitas of the Nonne Preestes Tale. MAE, 28, 1959, 172-79.

SZÖVÉRFFY, JOSEPH. "Roma" and "Anglia": Survival of a Poetic Image. NQ, 7, 1960, 248-50.

The background of the apostrophe to "Gaufred" in NPT (3347ff.).

THE SECOND NUN'S PROLOGUE AND TALE

See Griffith, pp. 239-41.

REILLY, CYRIL A. Chaucer's Second Nun's Tale: Tiburce's Visit to Pope Urban. MLN, 69, 1954, 37-39.

THE CANON'S YEOMAN'S PROLOGUE AND TALE

See Griffith, pp. 241-42.

BALDWIN, R. G. The Yeoman's Canons: A Conjecture. JEGP, 61, 1962, 232-33.
GRENNEN, JOSEPH EDWARD. Jargon Transmuted: Alchemy in Chaucer's Canon's Yeoman's Tale. DA, 22, 859. Fordham Univ, 1960.
----------. The Canon's Yeoman and the Cosmic Furnace: Language and Meaning in the Canon's Yeoman's Tale. Crit, 4, 1962, 225-40.
----------. Chaucer's "Secree of Secrees": An Alchemical "Topic." PQ, 42, 1963, 562-66.
HARTUNG, ALBERT E. Inappropriate Pointing in The Canon's Yeoman's Tale, G1236-1239. PMLA, 77, 1962, 508-9.
HERZ, JUDITH SCHERER. The Canon's Yeoman's Prologue and Tale. MP, 58, 1961, 231-37.
ROSENBERG, BRUCE A. Swindling Alchemist, Antichrist. CRAS, 6, 1962, 566-80.

THE MANCIPLE'S PROLOGUE AND TALE

See Griffith, pp. 243-44.

BIRNEY, EARLE. Chaucer's "Gentil" Manciple and His "Gentil" Tale. NM, 61, 1960, 257-67.

DONNER, MORTON. The Unity of Chaucer's Manciple Frag-
ment. MLN. 70, 1955, 245-49.
ELLIOTT, J. D. The Moral of the Manciple's Tale. NQ, 1,
1954, 511-12.
HAZLETON, RICHARD. The Manciple's Tale: Parody and
Critique. JEGP, 62, 1963, 1-31.
LUMIANSKY, R. M. Chaucer's Cook-Host Relationship.
Med Stud, 17, 1955, 208-9.
REIDT, T. B. W. The She-Wolf's Mate. MAE, 24, 1955,
16-19.
ManT, 79ff.
SPECTOR, ROBERT DONALD. Chaucer's The Manciple's
Tale. NQ, 4, 1957, 26.

THE PARSON'S PROLOGUE AND TALE

See Griffith, pp. 244-46.

ACKERMAN, ROBERT W. "Pared out of Paper": Gawain
802 and Purity 1408. JEGP, 56, 1957, 410-17.
Reference to "bake-metes . . . castelled with papir"
(ParsT, 444).
BIGGINS, D(ENNIS). Chaucer: CT. X (I), 42-46. PQ, 42,
1963, 558-62.
FOX, ROBERT C. Chaucer and Aristotle. NQ, 5, 1958,
523-24.
Identifies the "philosophre" in ParsT, 484, as Aristotle.
----------. The Philosophre of Chaucer's Parson. MLN,
75, 1960, 101-2.
HAZELTON, RICHARD. Chaucer's Parson's Tale and the
Moralium Dogma Philosophorum. Traditio, 16, 1960,
255-74.
KELLOGG, A. L. , and ERNEST W. TALBERT. The Wy-
clifite Pater Noster and Ten Commandments. BJRL, 42,
1959-60, 345ff.
OWEN, CHARLES A. , JR. Relationship Between the Physician's Tale and the Parson's Tale. MLN, 71, 1956,
84-87.

CHAUCER'S RETRACTION

See Griffith, pp. 246-47.

GORDON, JAMES D. Chaucer's Retraction: A Review of
  Opinion. Pp. 81-96 in Studies in Medieval Literature,
  edited by MacEdward Leach. Philadelphia: Univ of Pennsylvania Press; London: Oxford Univ Press, 1961.
  See section General Criticism under the name of the
  editor for a description of this volume.
LUMIANSKY, R. M. Chaucer's Retraction and the Degree
  of Completeness of the Canterbury Tales. TSE, 6, 1956,
  5-13.
MADDEN, WILLIAM A. Chaucer's Retraction and Mediaeval Canons of Seemliness. Med Stud, 17, 1955, 173-84.

WORKS OTHER THAN
THE CANTERBURY TALES: GENERAL
INCLUDING APOCRYPHA

See Griffith, pp. 248-51.

BETHURUM, DOROTHY. Chaucer's Point of View as Narrator in the Love Poems. PMLA, 74, 1959, 511-20.
   A discussion of the narrator in BD, HF, PF, the Prologue to LGW and Troilus and Criseyde; reprinted in Schoeck and Taylor, Eds., Chaucer Criticism, Vol. II.
CARTER, THOMAS H. The Shorter Poems of Geoffrey Chaucer. Shen, 11, 1960, 48-60.
FRIEDMAN, ALBERT B. Late Mediaeval Ballade and Origin of Broadside Balladry. MAE, 27, 1958, 95-110.
   Chaucer's use of the ballade form.
GREEN, A. WIGFALL. Chaucer's Complaints: Stanzaic Arrangement, Meter, and Rhyme. UMSE, 3, 1962, 19-34.
----------. Structure of Three Minor Poems by Chaucer. UMSE, 4, 1963, 79-82.
   The three poems are : Truth, Gentilesse, and Lak of Stedfastnesse.
LAWLOR, JOHN. Piers Plowman: An Essay in Criticism. London: Edward Arnold; New York: Barnes and Noble, 1962.
   See Chapter vii ("The Poet and the Dreamer"), esp.

pp. 286-91, for a discussion of the dreamer-narrator in Chaucer.

SCHOECK, RICHARD J. , and JEROME TAYLOR, Eds. Chaucer Criticism. Vol. II: Troilus and Criseyde and the Minor Poems. Notre Dame, Ind. : Univ of Notre Dame Press, 1961.
See section General Criticism for a description of this work.

ANELIDA AND ARCITE

See Griffith, pp. 253-54.

GREEN, A. WIGFALL. Meter and Rhyme in Chaucer's Anelida and Arcite. UMSE, 2, 1961, 55-63.
SPEHAR, ELIZABETH MARIE. Chaucer's Anelida and Arcite: A New Edition. DA, 23, 1010. Univ of Colorado, 1962.

ASTROLABE

See Griffith, pp. 254-55.

CROSS, J. E. Teaching Method, 1391: Notes on Chaucer's Astrolabe. English, 10, 1955, 172-75.
FREEDMAN, WILLIAM A. Geoffrey Chaucer, Technical Writer. Journal of the Society of Technical Writers and Publishers, 7, 1961, 14-15.

BOETHIUS

See Griffith, pp. 256-60.

GREEN, RICHARD H. , Trans. Boethius: Consolation of Philosophy. New York: The Bobbs-Merrill Co. , 1962. (The Library of Liberal Arts, 86.)
HOLLANDER, JOHN. "Moedes or Prolaciouns" in Chaucer's Boece. MLN, 71, 1956, 397-99.

KOTTLER, BARNET. The Vulgate Tradition of the Conso-
latio Philosophiae in the Fourteenth Century. Med Stud,
17, 1955, 209-14.

BOOK OF THE DUCHESS

See Griffith, pp. 260-62.

BAKER, DONALD C. The Dreamer again in The Book of the
Duchess. PMLA, 70, 1955, 279-82.
----------. Imagery and Structure in Chaucer's Book of the
Duchess. SN, 30, 1958, 17-26.
BEICHNER, PAUL E. The Medieval Representative of Mu-
sic, Jubal or Tubalcain? Notre Dame, Ind.: Univ of Notre
Dame Press, 1954. (Texts and Studies in the History of
Medieval Education, 2.)
    References to BD.
CRAMPTON, GEORGIA RONAN. Transitions and Meaning
in The Book of the Duchess. JEGP, 62, 1963, 486-500.
FRENCH, W. H. The Man in Black's Lyric. JEGP, 56,
1957, 231-41.
FURNIVALL, F. J., Ed. The Booke of the Duchesse, Made
by Geffrey Chawcyer at the Request of the Duke of Lancas-
tar, Pitiously Complaynynge the Deathe of the Sayd
Duchesse Blanche. Lexington, Ky.: Anvil Press, 1954.
    See section entitled Manuscripts for a description of
this volume.
HUPPÉ, BERNARD F., and D. W. ROBERTSON, JR. Fruyt
and Chaf: Studies in Chaucer's Allegories. Princeton,
N.J.: Princeton Univ Press, 1963.
    Allegorical interpretation of BD and PF.
LAWLOR, JOHN. The Pattern of Consolation in The Book of
the Duchess. Spec, 31, 1956, 626-48.
LUMIANSKY, R. M. The Bereaved Narrator in Chaucer's
The Book of the Duchess. TSE, 9, 1959, 5-17.
MANNING, STEPHEN. That Dreamer Once More. PMLA,
71, 1956, 540-41.
----------. Chaucer's Good Fair White: Woman and Symbol.
CL, 10, 1958, 97-105.

MORETON, REBECCA LARCHE. Literary Convention in
The Book of the Duchess. UMSE, 4, 1963, 69-78.
NAULT, CLIFFORD A., JR. "Foure and Twenty Yer"
Again. MLN, 71, 1956, 319-21.
ROWLAND, BERYL. The Chess Problem in Chaucer's
Book of the Duchess. Ang, 80, 1962, 384-89.
----------. "A Round Tour of Yvoyre" (The Book of the
Duchess, 946). NQ, 10, 1963, 9.
SCHAAR, CLAES. An Emendation in Chaucer's Book of the
Duchess. E Stud, 35, 1954, 16.
BD, 354-59.
SEVERS, J. BURKE. The Sources of The Book of the Duch-
ess. Med Stud, 25, 1963, 355-62.
STEADMAN, JOHN M. Chaucer's "Whelp": A Symbol of
Marital Fidelity? NQ, 3, 1956, 374-75.

COMPLAINT UNTO PITY

See Griffith, p. 263.

PITTOCK, MALCOLM. Chaucer: The Complaint unto Pity.
Crit, 1, 1959, 160-68.

COURT OF LOVE

See Griffith, p. 264.

FRASER, RUSSELL A. Ed. The Court of Venus. Durham,
N.C.: Duke Univ Press, 1955; London: Cambridge Univ
Press, 1956.
See section Editions with Notes for reviews.

THE EQUATORIE OF THE PLANETIS

Not in Griffith.

HERDAN, G. Chaucer's Authorship of The Equatorie of the
Planetis: The Use of Romance Vocabulary as Evidence.
Language, 32, 1956, 254-59.

KENNEDY, E. S. A Horoscope of Messehalla in the Chaucer Equatorium Manuscript. Spec, 34, 1959, 629-30.
PRICE, DEREK J., Ed. The Equatorie of the Planetis. With a Linguistic Analysis by R. M. Wilson. Cambridge Univ Press, 1955.
See section Editions with Notes for reviews.

FORMER AGE

See Griffith, p. 264.

NORTON-SMITH, J. Chaucer's Etas Prima. MAE, 32, 1963, 117-24.
PACE, GEORGE B. The True Text of The Former Age. Med Stud, 23, 1961, 363-67.

GAMELYN

See Griffith, p. 265.

ROGERS, FRANKLIN R. The Tale of Gamelyn and the Editing of The Canterbury Tales. JEGP, 58, 1959, 49-59.

HOUSE OF FAME

See Griffith, pp. 266-71.

ALLEN, ROBERT J. A Recurring Motif in Chaucer's House of Fame. JEGP, 55, 1956, 393-405.
BAKER, DONALD C. Recent Interpretations of Chaucer's Hous of Fame and a New Suggestion. UMSE, 1, 1960, 97-104.
    The "recent interpretations" are those by Allen, above, and by Ruggiers (SP, 50, 1953, 16-29); the Ruggiers article is reprinted in Schoeck and Taylor, Eds., Chaucer Criticism, Vol. II, pp. 261-74.
BEVINGTON, DAVID M. On Translating Ovid in Chaucer's House of Fame. NQ, 7, 1960, 206-7.
----------. The Obtuse Narrator in Chaucer's House of Fame. Spec, 36, 1961, 288-98.

BRUNNER, KARL. Chaucer's House of Fame. Actes du
    Cinquième Congrès International des Langues et Littéra-
    tures Modernes. Firenze, 1955, pp. 55-62.
CAWLEY, A. C. Chaucer, Pope, and Fame. REL, 3, 1962,
    9-19.
CIGADA, SERGIO. Il tema arturiano del "Château Tour-
    nant": Chaucer e Christine de Pisan. Studi Medievali,
    Fasc. 2, 1961, 576-606.
COLVERT, JAMES B. A Reference to Music in Chaucer's
    House of Fame. MLN, 69, 1954, 239-41.
    On the meaning of "cordes" in HF, 696.
DAVID, ALFRED. Literary Satire in the House of Fame.
    PMLA, 75, 1960, 333-39.
GOFFIN, R. C. "Tidings" in the Hous of Fame. NQ, 8,
    1961, 246.
HALL, LOUIS BREWER. Chaucer and the Dido-and-Aeneas
    Story. Med Stud, 25, 1963, 148-59.
KOONCE, BENJAMIN G. , JR. Chaucer and the Tradition of
    Fame: A Study of the Symbolism in The House of Fame.
    DA, 20, 3729-30. Princeton Univ, 1959.
LEWIS, R. W. B. On Translating the Aeneid: "Yif That I
    Can. " YCGL, 10, 1961, 7-15.
McCOLLUM, JOHN I. , JR. The House of Fame Revisited.
    A Chaucerian Puzzle and Other Medieval Essays, edited by
    N. G. Lawrence and J. A. Reynolds, pp. 71-85. Coral
    Gables, Florida: Univ of Miami Press, 1961.
MANZALAOUI, MAHMOUD A. Three Notes on Chaucer's
    Hous of Fame. NQ, 9, 1962, 85-86.
NEVILLE, MARIE. Chaucer and St. Clare. JEGP, 55,
    1956, 423-30.
    The Eagle's oath "by Seynte Clare" at line 1066.
RUGGIERS, PAUL G. Words into Images in Chaucer's
    Hous of Fame: A Third Suggestion. MLN, 69, 1954, 34-
    37.
    HF, 1068-81, and Paradiso, Canto 3.
SCHOECK, R. J. A Legal Reading of Chaucer's Hous of
    Fame. UTQ, 23, 1954, 185-92.
SOLARI, MARTA STELLA. Sources of the Invocation in the
    House of Fame. Revista de Literaturas Modernas (Mendo-
    za, Argentina), No. 1, 1956 (pub. 1957), 217-25.

STEADMAN, JOHN M. Chaucer's Eagle: A Contemplative
   Symbol. PMLA, 75, 1960, 153-59.
----------. "Goddes Boteler" and "Stellifye" (The Hous of
   Fame, 581, 592). Archiv, 197, 1960, 16-18.
----------. Chaucer's "Desert of Libye, " Venus, and Jove
   (The Hous of Fame, 486-87). MLN, 76, 1961, 196-201.
STILLWELL, GARDINER. Chaucer's "O Sentence" in the
   Hous of Fame. ES, 37, 1956, 149-57.
WILKINS, ERNEST H. Descriptions of Pagan Divinities
   from Petrarch to Chaucer. Spec, 32, 1957, 511-22.
WILLIAMS, GEORGE G. The Hous of Fame and the House
   of the Musicians. MLN, 72, 1957, 6-9.
WILSON, WILLIAM SMITH. Chaucer's House of Fame.
   Yale Univ Diss., 1961.

LEGEND OF GOOD WOMEN

See Griffith, pp. 272-82.

BAKER, DONALD C. Dreamer and Critic: the Poet in the
   Legend of Good Women. UCSLL, No. 9, 1963, pp. 4-18.
BRADLEY, D. R. Fals Eneas and Sely Dido. PQ, 39, 1960,
   122-25.
BROWN, CALVIN S. Yet Once More "for the Nones. " BUSE,
   3, 1957, 228-30.
HALL, LOUIS BREWER. Chaucer and the Dido-and-Aeneas
   Story. Med Stud, 25, 1963, 148-59.
KOONCE, BENJAMIN G. , JR. Satan the Fowler. Med Stud,
   21, 1959, 176-84.
LEACH, ELEANOR JANE WINSOR. The Sources and Rheto-
   ric of Chaucer's Legend of Good Women and Ovid's Hero-
   ides. Yale Univ Diss., 1963.
McLAUGHLIN, JOHN C. "The Honour and the Humble Obey-
   saunce": Prologue to The Legend of Good Women, L. 135,
   G-Text. PQ, 38, 1959, 515-16.
MONTGOMERY, MARION. "For the Nones" Once More.
   BUSE, 3, 1957, 177-78.
ROWLAND, BERYL. Chaucer's Daisy (Prol. LGW, F. 120-
   23; G. 109-11). NQ, 10, 1963, 210.

MARS

See Griffith, pp. 282-83.

BREWER, D. S. Chaucer's Complaint of Mars. NQ, 1,
1954, 462-63.
STILLWELL, GARDINER. Convention and Individuality in
Chaucer's Complaint of Mars. PQ, 35, 1956, 69-89.
WILLIAMS GEORGE G. What is the Meaning of Chaucer's
Complaint of Mars? JEGP, 57, 1958, 167-76.

PARLEMENT OF FOULES

See Griffith, pp. 284-88.

BAKER, DONALD C. The Poet of Love and the Parlement
of Foules. UMSE, 2, 1961, 79-110.
BENNETT, J. A. W. The Parlement of Foules: An Interpretation. Oxford: Clarendon Press; New York: Oxford
Univ Press, 1957.
    Rev: Dorothy Bethurum, Spec, 33, 1958, 263-65; TLS,
Jan 10, 1958, 16; Barbara M. H. Strang, DUJ, 19,
1958, 139-42; Ian Bishop, MAE, 27, 1958, 204-6; Nils
Erik Enkvist, MS, 53, 1959, 293-95; D. S. Brewer, RES,
10, 1959, 404-6; Guy Bourquin, EA, 12, 1959, 59-60;
Macdonald Emslie, EC, 9, 1959, 79-82; Theodore Silver-
stein, Chaucer's Modest and Homely Poem: The Parle-
ment, MP, 56, 1958-59, 270-76 (rev. art.); Przemyslaw
Mroczkowski, KN, No. 1, 1959, 64-67; J. B. Bessinger,
Chaucer: A Parliament of Critics, UTQ, 29, 1959-60,
91-96 (rev. art.).
BETHURUM, DOROTHY. The Center of the Parlement of
Foules. Essays in Honor of Walter Clyde Curry, pp. 39-
50. Nashville, Tenn.: Vanderbilt Univ Press, 1954.
BREWER, D. S. The Genre of the Parlement of Foules.
MLR, 53, 1958, 321-26.
----------, Ed. The Parlement of Foulys. London: Nelson;
New York: Barnes and Noble, 1960. (Nelson's Medieval
and Renaissance Library.)

Rev: Peter Dronke, NQ, 8, 1961, 475-76; J. A. Burrow,
RES, 12, 1961, 413-15; Dorothy Bethurum, MAE, 30,
1961, 195-98; Charles Muscatine, MLR, 57, 1962, 81-82.
----------, and F. W. BATESON. English in the University: III. Language and Literature. EC, 11, 1961, 243-63.

In an Editorial Appendix (pp. 255-63) to the essay by
Brewer, F. W. Bateson discusses the question of style
in Chaucer's poetry and illustrates his remarks by stylistic analysis of the 1st stanza of PF.

EMERSON, KATHERINE T. The Parlement of Foules and
Lionel of Clarence: A Reply. MAE, 26, 1957, 107-9.

A reply to the article by Ethel Seaton; see below in this
section; a rejoinder by Seaton follows (ibid., 109-11).

EMSLIE, MACDONALD. Codes of Love and Class Distinctions. EC, 5, 1955, 1-17.

This essay provoked the following responses, the 1st
three of which appeared in "The Critical Forum," ibid.,
405-18, under the title "Natural Love in The Parlement
of Foules": Cecily Clark (405-7); D. S. Brewer (407-13);
Macdonald Emslie (413-18). A final communication (by
D. S. Brewer) appeared in EC, 6, 1956, 248 under the
title "The Parlement of Foules." In the words of the
YWES reviewer, ". . . the viewpoints diverge so much
that resolution seems unlikely."

EVERETT, DOROTHY. Chaucer's Love Visions, with Particular Reference to the Parlement of Foules. Chapter iv
of Essays on Middle English Literature, edited by Patricia Kean. London: Oxford Univ Press, 1955.

Rev: A. C. Cawley, MLR, 51, 1956, 91-92.

FRANK, ROBERT WORTH, JR. Structure and Meaning in
the Parlement of Foules. PMLA, 71, 1956, 530-39.

FRIEDMAN, WILLIAM F., and ELIZABETH S. Acrostics,
Anagrams, and Chaucer. PQ, 38, 1959, 1-20.

A reply to the article by Ethel Seaton; see below in this
section.

HARRISON, THOMAS P. They Tell of Birds: Chaucer,
Spenser, Milton, Drayton. Austin, Texas: Univ of Texas
Press, 1956.

Rev: R. Bedichek, Southwestern Review, 42, 1957, 344-45.

HUPPÉ, BERNARD F., and D. W. ROBERTSON, JR. Fruyt and Chaf: Studies in Chaucer's Allegories. Princeton, N.J.: Princeton Univ Press, 1963.
Allegorical interpretation of BD and PF.

McDONALD, CHARLES O. An Interpretation of Chaucer's Parlement of Foules. Spec, 30, 1955, 444-57.
Reprinted in Schoeck and Taylor, Eds., Chaucer Criticism, Vol. II, pp. 275-93.

MANZALAOUI, MAHMOUD A. Ars Longa, Vita Brevis. EC, 12, 1962, 221-24.

RAYMO, R. R. The Parlement of Foules 309-15. MLN, 71, 1956, 159-60.

ROWLAND, BERYL. Chaucer's "Throstil Old" and Other Birds. Med Stud, 24, 1962, 381-84.
PF, 364.

SEATON, ETHEL. The Parlement of Foules and Lionel of Clarence. MAE, 25, 1956, 168-74.
See replies by Katherine T. Emerson (with rejoinder by Ethel Seaton) and by William F. and Elizabeth S. Friedman, above in this section.

STILLWELL, GARDINER. Chaucer's Eagles and Their Choice on February 14. JEGP, 53, 1954, 546-61.

THE ROMAUNT OF THE ROSE

See Griffith, pp. 290-93.

SUTHERLAND, RONALD. The Romaunt of the Rose and Source Manuscripts. PMLA, 74, 1959, 178-83.

----------. The Romaunt of the Rose and Le Roman de la Rose: a Parallel Text Edition. Wayne State Univ Diss., 1960.

VYVYAN, JOHN. Shakespeare and the Rose of Love: A Study of the Early Plays in Relation to the Medieval Philosophy of Love. London: Chatto and Windus; New York: Barnes and Noble, 1960.

TROILUS AND CRISEYDE

See Griffith, pp. 294-310.

ADAMS, JOHN F. Irony in Troilus' Apostrophe to the Vacant House of Criseyde. MLQ, 24, 1963, 61-65.

apROBERTS, ROBERT P. The Central Episode in Chaucer's Troilus. PMLA, 77, 1962, 373-85.

BASS, EBEN. The Jewels of Troilus. CE, 23, 1961-62, 145-47.

BAUGH, ALBERT C. , and E. TALBOT DONALDSON. Chaucer's Troilus, iv. 1585: A Biblical Allusion? MLN, 76, 1961, 1-4, 4-5.

   Replies to the article by L. G. Evans, below in this section.

BAYLEY, JOHN. The Characters of Love: A Study in the Literature of Personality. London: Constable, 1960; New York: Basic Books, 1961.

   See esp. Chapter ii: Love and the Code: Troilus and Criseyde (pp. 49-123).

   Rev: V. S. Pritchett, New Statesman, 61, 1961, 179-80; William Golding, Spect, Feb 10, 1961, 194; Graham Hough, List, 65, 1961, 459; TLS, Feb 24, 1961, 122; John Wain, Encounter, 17, 1961, 70-75; W. J. Harvey, EC, 12, 1962,95-97; D. S. Brewer, RES,13, 1962, 429-30.

BLOOMFIELD, MORTON W. Distance and Predestination in Troilus and Criseyde. PMLA, 72, 1957, 14-26.

   Reprinted in Schoeck and Taylor, Eds., Chaucer Criticism, Vol. II, pp. 196-210.

----------. The Eighth Sphere: A Note on Chaucer's Troilus and Criseyde, v, 1809. MLR, 53, 1958, 408-10.

BORTHWICK, SISTER MARY CHARLOTTE. Antigone's Song as "Mirour" in Chaucer's Troilus and Criseyde. MLQ, 22, 1961, 227-35.

BOWERS, R. H. The "Suttell and Dissayvabull" World of Chaucer's Troilus. NQ, 4, 1957, 278-79.

BREWER, D. S. Love and Marriage in Chaucer's Poetry. MLR, 49, 1954, 461-64.

CAMPBELL, JACKSON J. A New Troilus Fragment. PMLA, 73, 1958, 305-8.

See section Manuscripts for a description.

CASSIDY, FREDERIC G. "Don Thyn Hood" in Chaucer's
Troilus. JEGP, 57, 1958, 739-42.

T and C, II, 954.

COSTELLO, SISTER MARY ANGELICA. The Goddes and
God in the Troilus. DA, 23, 3352. Fordham Univ, 1962.

CRAIG, HARDIN. From Gorgias to Troilus. Pp. 97-107 in
Studies in Medieval Literature: In Honor of Professor
Albert Croll Baugh, edited by MacEdward Leach. Phila-
delphia: Univ of Pennsylvania Press; London: Oxford Univ
Press, 1961.

DALY, SARALYN R. Criseyde's Blasphemous Aube. NQ,
10, 1963, 442-44.

DAVID, ALFRED. The Hero of the Troilus. Spec, 37, 1962,
566-81.

D'EVELYN, CHARLOTTE. Pandarus a Devil? PMLA, 71,
1956, 275-79.

DOLAN, SISTER GRACE MARIA. The Narrator in Chaucer's
Troilus and Criseyde as an Example of the Point of View
Technique. St. John's Univ Diss., 1961.

DONALDSON, E. TALBOT. The Ending of Chaucer's Troilus. Pp. 26-45 in Early English and Norse Studies Presented to Hugh Smith in Honour of His Sixtieth Birthday,
edited by Arthur Brown and Peter Foote. London: Methu-
en, 1963.

DUNNING, T. P. God and Man in Troilus and Criseyde.
Pp. 164-82 in English and Medieval Studies Presented to
J. R. R. Tolkien on the Occasion of His Seventieth Birth-
day, edited by Norman Davis and C. L. Wrenn. London:
George Allen and Unwin, 1962.

EDMUNDS, PAUL E. A Defense of Chaucer's Diomede.
Classical Folia, 16, 1962, 110-23.

EVANS, LAWRENCE GOVE. A Biblical Allusion in Troilus
and Criseyde. MLN, 74, 1959, 584-87.

Suggests that T and C, IV, 1585, contains an allusion to
Matthew 10:39. See replies by E. Talbot Donaldson and
Albert C. Baugh, above in this section under Baugh.

EVERETT, DOROTHY. Troilus and Criseyde. Chapter v
of Essays on Middle English Literature, edited by Patricia Kean. London: Oxford Univ Press, 1955.

Rev: A. C. Cawley, MLR, 51, 1956, 91-92.

FOSTER, KENELM. Italy and the English Poets: Chaucer, Dante and Boccaccio. The Tablet, 206, 1955, 476-77.

FOWLER, DAVID C. An Unusual Meaning of "Win" in Chaucer's Troilus and Criseyde. MLN, 69, 1954, 313-15.
    T and C, I, 390.

GAYLORD, ALAN. Uncle Pandarus as Lady Philosophy. PMASAL, 46, 1961, 571-95.

GILL, SISTER BARBARA ANN. Paradoxical Patterns in Chaucer's Troilus: An Explanation of the Palinode. Washington, D. C.: The Catholic Univ of America Press, 1960.
    Rev: John Burrow, RES, 13, 1962, 326.

GNERRO, MARK L. "Ye, Haselwodes Shaken!"--Pandarus and Divination. NQ, 9, 1962, 164-65.

GREEN, MARION N. Christian Implications of Knighthood and Courtly Love in Chaucer's Troilus. Delaware Notes, 30, 1957, 57-92.

HAGOPIAN, JOHN V. Chaucer as Psychologist in Troilus and Criseyde. Literature and Psychology, 5, 1955, 5-11.

HUTSON, ARTHUR E. Troilus' Confession. MLN, 69, 1954, 468-70.

JELLIFFE, ROBERT ARCHIBALD. Troilus and Criseyde: Studies in Interpretation. Tokyo: The Hokuseido Press, 1956.

JOHNSTON, EVERETT C. The Pronoun of Address in Chaucer's Troilus. Language Quarterly, 1, 1962, 17-20.

JORDAN, ROBERT M. The Narrator in Chaucer's Troilus. ELH, 25, 1958, 237-57.

JOSEPH, BERTRAM. Troilus and Criseyde: "A Most Admirable and Inimitable Epicke Poeme." Essays and Studies, 7, 1954, 42-61.
    The subtitle comes from Sir Francis Kynaston's description of his Latin "version of Troilus and Criseyde (dated 1623) in the Bodleian."

KASKE, R. E. The Aube in Chaucer's Troilus. Pp. 167-79 in Chaucer Criticism, edited by Richard J. Schoeck and Jerome Taylor, Vol. II: Troilus and Crissida and The Minor Poems. Notre Dame, Ind.: Univ of Notre Dame Press, 1961.

KELLOGG, ALFRED L. On the Tradition of Troilus's
  Vision of the Little Earth. Med Stud, 22, 1960, 204-13.
KIRBY, T. A. Chaucer's Troilus. Gloucester, Mass.:
  Peter Smith, 1959. Reprint.
  A reprint of the original ed. of 1940; see Griffith,
  p. 301, for reviews.
KLEINSTÜCK, JOHANNES WALTER. Chaucers Troilus und
  die höfische Liebe. Archiv, 193, 1956, 1-14.
KORNBLUTH, ALICE FOX. Another Chaucer Pun. NQ, 6,
  1959, 243.
  T and C, IV, 312: "stonden for naught. "
KREUZER, JAMES R. The Zanis Quotation in Chaucer's
  Troilus and Criseyde, IV, 415. NQ, 4, 1957, 237.
LEVER, KATHERINE. The Christian Classicist's Dilemma.
  CJ, 58, 1963, 356-61.
  T and C, III, 930-31: "I am . . . At dulcarnoun. "
LONGO, JOSEPH A. The Double Time Scheme in Book II
  of Chaucer's Troilus and Criseyde. MLQ, 22, 1961,
  37-40.
LUMIANSKY, R. M. Calchas in the Early Versions of the
  Troilus Story. TSE, 4, 1954, 5-20.
  See the section Literary Relations and Sources for a
  number of articles by R. M. Lumiansky which deal with
  earlier versions of the Troilus story.
McCALL, JOHN P. Classical Myth in Chaucer's Troilus
  and Criseyde: An Aspect of the Classical Tradition in the
  Middle Ages. DA, 17, 1329-30. Princeton Univ, 1955.
----------, and GEORGE RUDISILL, JR. The Parliament
  of 1386 and Chaucer's Trojan Parliament. JEGP, 58,
  1959, 276-88.
----------. Chaucer's May 3. MLN, 76, 1961, 201-5.
----------. Five-Book Structure in Chaucer's Troilus.
  MLQ, 23, 1962, 297-308.
----------. The Trojan Scene in Chaucer's Troilus. ELH,
  29, 1962, 263-75.
MacKAY, ELEANOR MAXINE. The Clash and the Fusion of
  Medieval and Renaissance Elements in Chaucer's Troilus.
  DA, 19, 2615-16. Emory Univ, 1958.
MAGOUN, FRANCIS P., JR. Chaucer's Summary of Sta-
  tius' Thebaid II-XII. Traditio, 11, 1955, 409-20.

MALARKEY, STODDARD. The Corones Tweyne: An Interpretation. Spec, 38, 1963, 473-78.

MEECH, SANFORD B. Design in Chaucer's Troilus. Syracuse, N.Y.: Syracuse Univ Press, 1959.
Rev: Morton W. Bloomfield, MLN, 75, 1960, 431-34; John Burrow, RES, 11, 1960, 314-16; E. M. Clark, BA, 34, 1960, 295; Thomas A. Kirby, JEGP, 59, 1960, 567-69; Francis Lee Utley, Spec, 35, 1960, 313-19; Stanley B. Greenfield, CL, 12, 1960, 360-61.

MORAN, TATYANA. The Testament of Cresseid and The Book of Troylus. Litera, 6, 1959, 18-24.

MUDRICK, MARVIN. Chaucer's Nightingales. Hudson Reiew, 10, 1957, 88-95.

MUSTANOJA, TAUNO F. Troilus and Criseyde, IV, 607; "Of Fered." NM, 56, 1955, 174-77.

NAGARAJAN, S. The Conclusion to Chaucer's Troilus and Criseyde. EC, 13, 1963, 1-8.

NOJIMA, HIDEKATSU. Four Cressidas--A Heroine in Eclipse: Part I, Chaucer's Cressida. Essays, No. 17, 1963, 50-81.
In Japanese; for an abstract in English, see AES, 7, 1964, Item 1352.

O'CONNOR, JOHN J. The Astronomical Dating of Chaucer's Troilus. JEGP, 55, 1956, 556-62.

OWEN, CHARLES A., JR. Chaucer's Method of Composition. MLN, 72, 1957, 164-65.

----------. The Significance of Chaucer's Revisions of Troilus and Criseyde. MP, 55, 1957-58, 1-5.

----------. The Significance of a Day in Troilus and Criseyde. Med Stud, 22, 1960, 366-70.

PATCH, HOWARD R. Two Notes on Chaucer's Troilus. MLN, 70, 1955, 8-12.
T and C, II, 1735-36; V, 638-41.

PRATT, ROBERT A. Chaucer and Le Roman de Troyle et de Criseida. SP, 53, 1956, 509-39.

RENOIR, ALAIN. Thebes, Troy, Criseyde, and Pandarus: An Instance of Chaucerian Irony. SN, 32, 1960, 14-17.

----------. Criseyde's Two Half Lovers. OL, 16, 1961, 239-55.

SAINTONGE, CONSTANCE. In Defense of Criseyde. MLQ,
    15, 1954, 312-20.
SCHLAUCH, MARGARET. Troilus i Kressyda Szekspira i
    Chaucera--Jezyk Metaforyczny w Swietle Przemian
    Spolecznych. KN, 1, 1954, 3-19.
----------. Antecedents of the English Novel 1400-1600
    (from Chaucer to Deloney). Warszwa: PWN-Polish Scien-
    tific Publishers; London: Oxford Univ Press, 1963.
    See esp. Chapter ii, Part IV (pp. 28-40): The Achieve-
    ment of Chaucer's Troilus and Criseyde.
SCOTT, FORREST S. The Seventh Sphere: A Note on Troi-
    lus and Criseyde. MLR, 51, 1956, 2-5.
SHARROCK, ROGER. Second Thoughts: C. S. Lewis on
    Chaucer's Troilus. EC, 8, 1958, 123-37.
SLAUGHTER, EUGENE E. Love and Grace in Chaucer's
    Troilus. Pp. 61-76 in Essays in Honor of Walter Clyde
    Curry. Nashville, Tenn.: Vanderbilt Univ Press, 1954.
SMYSER, H. M. The Domestic Background of Troilus and
    Criseyde. Spec, 31, 1956, 297-315.
SPEARING, A. C. The Testament of Cresseid and the "High
    Concise Style." Spec, 37, 1962, 208-25.
    References to style in T and C.
STEADMAN, JOHN M. The Age of Troilus. MLN, 72, 1957,
    89-90.
THOMPSON, LOUIS FELSINGER. Artistry in Troilus and
    Criseyde: A Study of Chronology, Structure, Characteri-
    zation, and Purpose. DA, 20, 1771. Lehigh Univ, 1959.
THOMSON, PATRICIA. The "Canticus Troili": Chaucer
    and Petrarch. CL, 11, 1959, 313-28.
UTLEY, FRANCIS LEE. Scene-Division in Chaucer's Troi-
    lus and Criseyde. Pp. 109-38 in Studies in Medieval Liter-
    ature, edited by MacEdward Leach. Philadelphia: Univ
    of Pennsylvania Press; London: Oxford Univ Press, 1961.
WILLIAMS, GEORGE G. Who Were Troilus, Criseyde, and
    Pandarus? The Rice Institute Pamphlet, 44, 1957, 126-
    46.
----------. The Troilus and Criseyde Frontispiece Again.
    MLR, 57, 1962, 173-78.

GENERAL BACKGROUNDS
INCLUDING HISTORICAL
AND PHILOSOPHIC BACKGROUNDS

See Griffith, pp. 314-29.

AUERBACH, ERICH. Literatursprache und Publikum in der lateinischen Spätantike und im Mittelalter. Bern: Francke Verlag, 1958.
  Rev: Edward Charles Witke, Spec, 34, 1959, 440-43.
BLAIR, CLAUDE. European Armour circa 1066 to circa 1700. London: Batsford, 1958; New York: Macmillan, 1959.
  Rev: Urban T. Holmes, Jr., Spec, 35, 1960, 428-30.
BREWER, DEREK. Chaucer in His Time. London: T. Nelson, 1963.
BROWN, R. ALLEN. English Medieval Castles. (The New Heritage Series.) London: Batsford, 1954.
  Rev: TLS, Jan 21, 1955, 42.
CHRIMES, STANLEY BERTRAM. An Introduction to the Administrative History of Mediaeval England. 2nd rev. ed. (Studies in Mediaeval History, 7.) Oxford: Blackwell, 1959.
----------, and A. L. BROWN. Select Documents of English Constitutional History, 1307-1485. London: A. and C. Black; New York: Barnes and Noble, 1961.
  Rev: TLS, March 24, 1961, 183.

COULTON, G. G. The Medieval Scene: An Informal Intro-
duction to the Middle Ages. Cambridge Univ Press, 1959.
(Cambridge Paperbacks.)
   Reprint of the 1st ed. (1930); see Griffith, p. 317, for
reviews.
----------. Medieval Panorama: The English Scene from
Conquest to Reformation. New York: The Noonday Press
(Meridian Books), 1955; London: Collins, 1961.
   See Griffith, p. 318, for notice of 1st ed. (1938) and
numerous reviews.
----------. Medieval Village, Manor and Monastery. New
York: Harper (Torchbooks); London: Hamilton, 1960.
   First printed in 1925 under the title The Medieval Vil-
lage; see Griffith, p. 317.
----------. Chaucer and His England. With a New Bibli-
ography by T. W. Craik. London: Methuen; New York:
Barnes and Noble, 1963. (Univ Paperbacks, UP 46.)
   See Griffith, p. 317, for notice of the 1st (1908) and
subsequent eds. of this book; also reviews.
DALY, LOWRIE JOHN. The Political Theory of John Wy-
clif. (Jesuit Studies: Contributions to the Arts and Sci-
ences by Members of the Society of Jesus.) Chicago:
Loyola Univ Press, 1962.
DAVIS, G. R. C. Medieval Cartularies of Great Britain:
A Short Catalogue. London and New York: Longmans,
Green, 1958.
   Rev: M. D. Knowles, Library, 13, 1958, 300-1; His-
tory Today, 8, 1958, 364.
DOWNS, NORTON, Ed. Basic Documents in Medieval His-
tory. Princeton, N.J., and London: D. Van Nostrand,
1959. (Anvil Books, 38.)
DUCKETT, ELEANOR SHIPLEY. The Gateway to the Middle
Ages. 3 vols.: Italy; France and Britain; Monasticism.
2nd rev. ed. Ann Arbor: Univ of Michigan Press (Ann
Arbor Paperbacks, AA 50, 51, 52); London: Cresset
Press, 1961.
   See Griffith, p. 319, for reviews of the 1st ed. (1938).
HASKINS, C. H. Studies in Mediaeval Culture. London: Con-
stable; New York: F. Ungar, 1958.

Reprint of the 1st ed. (1929); see Griffith, p. 321, for
reviews.
HASTINGS, MARGARET. High History or Hack History:
England in the Later Middle Ages. Spec, 36, 1961, 225-
53.
Rev: W. Lammers, Historische Zeitschrift, 193 (Heft
3), 1961, 739.
HEER, FRIEDRICH. Mittelalter. Zürich: Kindler Verlag,
1961.
----------. The Medieval World: Europe from 1100-1350.
Trans. from the German by Janet Sondheimer. London:
Weidenfeld and Nicolson; Cleveland and New York: World
Pub. Co., 1962.
Rev: TLS, July 13, 1962, 507; Alan Bennett, New
Statesman, 64, 1962, 876; Eleanor S. Duckett, NYTB,
Sept 2, 1962, 10-11; Sidney R. Packard, Spec, 38, 1963,
356-59.
HOLMES, GEORGE. The Later Middle Ages, 1272-1485.
(History of England Series.) London: T. Nelson, 1962.
INSTITUTE OF HISTORICAL RESEARCH (BIBLIOGRAPHY).
See under the names of the compilers, Joan C. Lancas-
ter (for the years 1946-1956) and William Kellaway (for
1957-1960).
JUSSERAND, J. J. English Wayfaring Life in the Middle
Ages. New ed. London: Methuen, 1961.
See Griffith, p. 322, for reviews of the ed. of 1920.
KANTOROWICZ, ERNST H. The King's Two Bodies: A Stu-
dy in Mediaeval Political Theology. Princeton, N.J.:
Princeton Univ Press; London: Oxford Univ Press, 1958.
Rev: William Huse Dunham, Jr., Spec, 33, 1958, 550-
53; F. M. Powicke, MAE, 28, 1959, 50-53; TLS, Nov 13,
1959, 665.
KELLAWAY, WILLIAM, Comp. Bibliography of Historical
Works Issued in the United Kingdom, 1957-60. London:
Univ of London Institute of Historical Research, 1962.
A continuation of Joan C. Lancaster, Bibliography of
Historical Works . . . 1946-1956; see below under name
of compiler.
KNOWLES, DOM DAVID. The Evolution of Medieval

Thought. London: Longmans, Green; Baltimore, Md.: Helicon Press, 1962.

Rev: TLS, Oct 12, 1962, 796.

LANCASTER, JOAN C., Comp. Bibliography of Historical Works Issued in the United Kingdom, 1946-56. London: Univ of London Institute of Historical Research, 1957.

A continuation is listed above, under the name of the compiler, William Kellaway.

LEFF, GORDON. Bradwardine and the Pelagians: A Study of His De Causa Dei and Its Opponents. (Medieval Life and Thought, 5.) Cambridge Univ Press, 1957.

Rev: Ernest A. Moody, Spec, 33, 1958, 102-5; Aubrey Gwynn, MAE, 27, 1958, 200-3.

----------. Medieval Thought: St. Augustine to Ockham. Harmondsworth, England, and Baltimore, Md.: Penguin Books, 1958.

Rev: TLS, July 11, 1958, 387; S. Harrison Thomson, Spec, 35, 1960, 469-71.

----------. The Changing Pattern of Thought in the Earlier Fourteenth Century. BJRL, 43, 1961, 354-72.

LERNER, RALPH, and MUHSIN MAHDI, Eds. Medieval Political Philosophy: A Sourcebook. New York: The Free Press of Glencoe (Macmillan), 1963.

LEWIS, EWART, Ed. and Trans. Medieval Political Ideas. 2 vols. New York: Knopf; London: Routledge and Kegan Paul, 1954.

Rev: TLS, Oct 15, 1954, 655; Arthur A. North, Thought, 30, 1955, 296-98; Beryl Smalley, MAE, 24, 1955, 46-49; J. P. Duncan, BA, 30, 1956, 336-37.

LUBAC, HENRI DE. Exégèse Médiévale: Les Quatres Sens de l'Écriture. 2 vols. Paris: Aubier, 1959, 1961.

LYON, B. A. A Constitutional and Legal History of Medieval England. New York: Harper; London: H. Hamilton, 1960.

McKISACK, MAY. The Fourteenth Century, 1307-1399. (Oxford History of England, Vol. V.) Oxford: Clarendon Press, 1959.

Rev: TLS, Nov 6, 1959, 644; Maurice Ashley, List, 62, 1959, 695; Geoffrey Barraclough, Spect, Nov 6, 1959,

p. 639; J. O. Prestwich, New Statesman, 58, 1959, 887;
Y. Renouard, EHR, 77, 1962, 525-30.

MILNE, ALEXANDER TAYLOR, Comp.
See below in this section under ROYAL HISTORICAL
SOCIETY.

MORRALL, JOHN B. Political Thought in Medieval Times.
London: Hutchinson, 1958; 2nd ed., 1960. New York:
Harper, 1962 (Torchbooks, 1076).
Rev: Marshall W. Baldwin, Spec, 38, 1963, 142-43.

MUNDY, JOHN H. and PETER RIESENBERG. The Mediaeval Town. Princeton, N.J., and London: Van Nostrand,
1958. (An Anvil Original, 30.)

MURPHY, JAMES J. The Medieval Arts of Discourse: An
Introductory Bibliography. Speech Monographs, 29, 1962,
71-78.

NYKROG, PER. Les Fabliaux: Étude d'Histoire Littéraire
et de Stylistique Médiévale. Copenhagen: Einar Munksgaard, 1957.
Rev: Charles H. Livingston, Spec, 33, 1958, 310-16.

O'NEIL, B. H. St. J. Castles and Cannon: A Study of Early
Artillery Fortifications in England. Oxford: Clarendon
Press; New York: Oxford Univ Press, 1960.

PAINTER, SIDNEY. A History of the Middle Ages, 284-
1500. 2 vols. New York: Knopf; London: Macmillan,
1955.
Rev: TLS, March 25, 1955, 184.

PARKS, GEORGE B. The English Traveler to Italy. Vol. I:
The Middle Ages (to 1525). Rome: Edizioni di Storia e
Letteratura; Stanford, Calif.: Stanford Univ Press, 1954.

POOLE, A. L., Ed. Medieval England. (A new ed., in 2
vols., rewritten and revised.) Oxford: Clarendon Press;
New York: Oxford Univ Press, 1958.
Nineteen Chapters by various authorities in which are
discussed such subjects as "Heraldry" (by A. R. Wagner),
"Towns and Trade" (by E. M. Carus-Wilson), etc. This
volume is a successor to Medieval England, edited in
1924 by H. W. C. Davis; see Griffith, p. 319.
Rev: R. R. Bolgar, Cambridge Review, 80, 1959, 259,
261; TLS, Jan 23, 1959, 50; M. M. Postan and reply
by reviewer, ibid., Feb 13, 1959, 83; Donald W.

Sutherland, Spec, 34, 1959, 497-500; J. A. W. B(ennett), MAE, 31, 1962, 224-26.

POOLE, REGINALD L. Illustrations of the History of Medieval Thought and Learning. 2nd rev. ed. London: Constable; New York: Peter Smith, 1961.

See Griffith, p. 324, for notice of this ed., which was originally published in 1921.

POWICKE, MICHAEL. Military Obligation in Medieval England: A Study in Liberty and Duty. Oxford: Clarendon Press; New York: Oxford Univ Press, 1962.

Rev: Helen M. Cam, Spec, 38, 1963, 147-49.

QUADLBAUER, FRANZ. Die antike Theorie der genera dicendi im lateinischen Mittelalter. (Osterreichische Akademie der Wissenschaften.) Vienna: Hermann Böhlaus Nachf., 1962.

RICKERT, EDITH, Comp. Chaucer's World. Ed. by Clair C. Olson and Martin M. Crow. Illustrations Selected by Margaret Rickert. New York and London: Columbia Univ Press, 1962. (A Galaxy Edition.)

See Griffith, p. 324 under Olson, for notice and reviews of the 1st ed. (1948).

Rev: Margaret Galway, MLR, 58, 1963, 311.

RIESENBERG, PETER N. Inalienability of Sovereignty in Medieval Political Thought. (Columbia Studies in the Social Sciences, 591.) New York: Columbia Univ Press, Press, 1956.

Rev: Walter Ullmann, MAE, 26, 1957, 201-4; S. B. Chrimes, Hist, 42, 1957, 226-27.

ROBSON, J. A. Wyclyf and the Oxford Schools: The Relation of the Summa de ente to Scholastic Debates at Oxford in the later Fourteenth Century. (Cambridge Studies in Medieval Life and Thought, 8.) Cambridge and New York: Cambridge Univ Press, 1961.

Rev: S. Harrison Thomson, Spec, 38, 1963, 497-99.

ROYAL HISTORICAL SOCIETY. Writings on British History, 1940-1945. A Bibliography of Books and Articles on the History of Great Britain from about 400 A.D. to 1914, Published during the Years 1940-45 Inclusive, with an Appendix Containing a Select List of Publications in these Years on British History since 1914. Compiled by

Alexander Taylor Milne. 2 vols. London: Jonathan Cape, 1960.

RUSSELL, P. E. The English Intervention in Spain and Portugal in the Time of Edward III and Richard II. Oxford: Clarendon Press, 1955.

STEPHENSON, CARL. Medieval History: Europe from the Second to the Sixteenth Centuries. (The Harper Historical Series.) New York: Harper; London: Hamilton, 1962.

STRAYER, JOSEPH REESE, and DANA CARLETON MUNRO. The Middle Ages, 395-1500. 4th ed. New York: Appleton-Century-Crofts; London: Bell, 1959. (The Century Historical Series.)

   Revision of the volume by D. C. Munro entitled The Middle Ages, 395-1272, pub. in 1921; see Griffith, p. 323.

THOMPSON, JAMES WESTFALL. Economic and Social History of Europe in the Later Middle Ages (1300-1530). London: Constable; New York: F. Ungar, 1960.

   Reprint of the ed. of 1931; see Griffith, p. 327.

----------. The Medieval Library. Reprinted with a Supplement by Blanch B. Boyer. New York: Hafner, 1957.

   See Griffith, pp. 327-28, for reviews of the 1st ed. (1939).

TREVELYAN, GEORGE MACAULAY. England in the Age of Wycliffe, 1368-1520. Reprint. New York and Evanston, Ill.: Harper and Row, 1963. (Harper Torchbook, TB/1112.)

ULLMANN, WALTER. Principles of Government and Politics in the Middle Ages. New York: Barnes and Noble; London: Methuen, 1961.

UTLEY, FRANCIS L., Ed. The Forward Movement of the Fourteenth Century. (A Record of the 1958 Ohio State Medieval Conference with Lectures by George Cuttino, Hans Baron, Astrik Gabrial, Grace Frank, Alan Gewirth, and Harry Bober.) Columbus, Ohio: Ohio State Univ Press, 1961.

WARREN, W. L. The Peasants' Revolt of 1381. Part I: History Today, 12, 1962, 845-53. Part II: ibid., 13, 1963, 44-51.

WILKINSON, B. English Politics and Politicians of the

Thirteenth and Fourteenth Centuries. Spec, 30, 1955, 37-48.

----------. Constitutional History of Medieval England, 1216-1399. Vol. III: The Development of the Constitution, 1216-1399. London and New York: Longmans, Green, 1958.

Rev: TLS, March 14, 1958, 134; Arthur R. Hogue, Spec, 34, 1959, 344-46.

WILKS, MICHAEL J. Chaucer and the Mystical Marriage in Medieval Political Thought. BJRL, 44, 1962, 489-530.

----------. The Problem of Sovereignty in the Later Middle Ages: The Papal Monarchy with Augustinus Triumphus and the Publicists. (Cambridge Studies in Medieval Life and Thought, 9.) Cambridge and New York: Cambridge Univ Press, 1963.

SOCIAL BACKGROUNDS

See Griffith, pp. 330-42.

BAGLEY, JOHN J. Life in Medieval England. (English Life Series.) London: Batsford, 1960; New York: Putnam, 1961.
Rev: Dorothy Margaret Stuart, Hist Today, 10, 1960, 505-6.

BENTON, JOHN F. The Court of Champagne as a Literary Center. Spec, 36, 1961, 551-91.

----------. The Evidence for Andreas Capellanus Re-Examined Again. SP, 59, 1962, 471-78.
A critical review of the article by John F. Mahoney; see below in this section.

CHARLTON, JOHN. Life at a Medieval Court. List, 61, 1959, 886-87.

COHEN, JOHN M. A History of Western Literature. Harmondsworth, England, and Baltimore, Md.: Penguin Books, 1956. 2nd rev. ed.: London: Cassell, 1961. (The Belle Sauvage Library.)
See Chapter ii: "The Theme of Courtly Love."

DALY, L. J. The Medieval University, 1200-1400, With an Introduction by Pearl Kibre. London and New York: Sheed and Ward, 1961.

DENT, ANTHONY. Fair Burgesses. Hist Today, 11, 1961, 753-59.

DODD, WILLIAM GEORGE. Courtly Love in Chaucer and
Gower. Gloucester, Mass.: Peter Smith, 1958.
Reprint of the original ed. (1913); see Griffith, pp. 84-
85, for reviews.

DOYLE, A. I. The Social Context of Medieval English
Literature. A Guide to English Literature: The Age of
Chaucer, pp. 68-105. Edited by Boris Ford. Harmondsworth, England, and Baltimore, Md.: Penguin Books,
1954.

FERGUSON, ARTHUR B. The Indian Summer of English
Chivalry: Studies in the Decline and Transformation of
Chivalric Idealism. Durham, N. C.: Duke Univ Press,
1960.

HEERS, JACQUES. L'Occident aux XIVe et XVe Siècles:
Aspects Économiques et Sociaux. (Nouvelle Clio: L'Histoire et ses Problèmes, 23) Paris: Presses Universitaires de France, 1963.

HILL, MARY C. The King's Messengers, 1199-1377: A
Contribution to the History of the Royal Household. Lon-
don: E. Arnold, 1961.
Rev: TLS, Aug 25, 1961, 570.

JACKSON, W. T. H. The De Amore of Andreas Capellanus
and the Practice of Love at Court. RR, 49, 1958, 243-51.

KIBRE, PEARL. Scholarly Privileges in the Middle Ages:
The Rights, Privileges, and Immunities of Scholars and
Universities at Bologna, Padua, Paris, and Oxford. Lon-
don: The Mediaeval Academy of America, 1961; Cam-
bridge, Mass.: Mediaeval Academy of America, 1962.
Rev: E. M. Powicke, Spec, 37, 1962, 629-30.

MAHONEY, JOHN F. The Evidence for Andreas Capellanus
in Re-Examination. SP, 55, 1958, 1-6.
See reply by John F. Benton, above in this section.

----------. Ovid and Medieval Courtly Love Poetry. Classical Folia, 15, 1961, 14-27.

MEADER, WILLIAM G. Courtship in Shakespeare: Its Rela-
tion to the Tradition of Courtly Love. New York: King's
Crown Press (Columbia Univ), 1954.
References to Chaucer.

MOORMAN, CHARLES. Courtly Love in Malory. ELH, 27,
1960, 163-73.

NOJIMA, HIDEKATSU. The Tradition of Courtly Love. Es-
   says, No. 16, 1963, 43-78.
   In Japanese; for an abstract in English, see AES, 7,
   1964, Item 1349.
PAINTER, SIDNEY. Mediaeval Society. Ithaca, N. Y.: Cor-
   nell Univ Press, 1957.
PARRY, JOHN J. The Art of Courtly Love of Andreas
   Capellanus with Introduction, Translation and Notes. New
   York: F. Ungar, 1959; London: Christopher Johnson,
   1961.
   Reprint of the original ed. (1941); see Griffith, pp. 336-
   37, for notice and reviews.
----------. The Art of Courtly Love of Andreas Capellanus.
   Edited and abridged by Frederick W. Locke. (Milestones
   of Thought in the History of Ideas.) New York: F. Ungar,
   1957.
PLUCKNETT, T. F. T. The Mediaeval Bailiff. London:
   Athlone Press, 1954.
SCAGLIONE, ALDO D. Nature and Love in the Late Middle
   Ages: An Essay on the Cultural Context of the Decameron.
   Berkeley: Univ of California Press, 1963.
SCHLÖSSER, FELIX. Andreas Capellanus: Seine Minne-
   lehre und das christliche Weltbild um 1200. (Abhandlungen
   zur Kunst- Musik- und Literaturwissenschaft, 15.) Bonn:
   H. Bouvier, 1960.
THOMPSON, JAMES WESTFALL. The Literacy of the Laity
   in the Middle Ages. (Burt Franklin Research and Source
   Works Series, 2.) New York: Burt Franklin, 1960.
   Reprint of the original ed. (1939); see Griffith, p. 328,
   for reviews.
WEIGAND, HERMANN J. Three Chapters on Courtly Love
   in Arthurian France and Germany. (Univ of North Carolina Studies in the Germanic Languages and Literatures,
   17.) Chapel Hill: Univ of North Carolina Press, 1956.
   See esp. Chapter ii: Andreas Capellanus: De Amore.

ECONOMIC BACKGROUNDS

See Griffith, pp. 343-45.

ADELSON, HOWARD L. Medieval Commerce. Princeton, N.J., and London: D. Van Nostrand, 1962. (Anvil Books, 60.)

BAKER, DONALD C. Gold Coins in Mediaeval English Literature. Spec, 36, 1961, 282-87.

BAKER, ROBERT LEWIS. The Establishment of the English Wool Staple in 1313. Spec, 31, 1956, 444-53.

----------. The English Customs Service, 1307-1343: A Study of Medieval Administration. (Trans. of the American Philosophical Society, N.S. Vol. LI, Part VI.) Philadelphia, Pa.: American Philosophical Society, 1961.

Rev: Michael R. Powicke, Spec, 37, 1962, 407.

BERESFORD, MAURICE W. The Lost Villages of England. New York: Philosophical Library; London: Lutterworth Press, 1954.

Deals with the depopulation of mediaeval villages during the fifteenth century.

Rev: George Caspar Homans, Spec, 30, 1955, 250-52.

----------, and J. K. St. JOSEPH. Medieval England: An Aerial Survey. Cambridge Univ Press, 1958.

Rev: W. G. Hoskins, List, 59, 1958, 466; NQ, 5, 1958, 365-66; TLS, April 25, 1958, 223; Helmut Jäger, Historische Zeitschrift, 191, 1960, 151-54.

BRIDBURY, A. R. England and the Salt Trade in the Later
   Middle Ages. Oxford: Clarendon Press; New York: Oxford
   Univ Press, 1955.
      Rev: W. H. Chaloner, Hist Today, 5, 1955, 350-51;
   TLS, May 6, 1955, 234; Sylvia L. Thrupp, Spec, 31,
   1956, 139-40.
----------. Economic Growth: England in the Later Middle
   Ages. London: Allen and Unwin, 1962.
CARUS-WILSON, E. M. Medieval Merchant Venturers. Lon-
   don: Methuen, 1954.
      Rev: Sylvia L. Thrupp, Spec, 30, 1955, 467.
----------, and OLIVE COLEMAN. England's Export Trade
   1275-1547. Oxford: Clarendon Press; New York: Oxford
   Univ Press, 1963.
DOLLEY, R. H. M. Medieval Gold Coins from the Lockett
   Collection. BMQ, 21, 1957, 41-44.
DUBY, GEORGE. L'Économie Rurale et la Vie des Cam-
   pagnes dans l'Occident Médiéval. 2 vols. Paris: Aubier,
   1962.
EKWALL, EILERT. Studies on the Population of Medieval
   London. (Kungl. Vitterhets-, Historie- och antikvitets-
   akademiens Handlingar. Filologisk-filosofiska Serien, 2.)
   Stockholm: Almqvist and Wiksell, 1956.
      Rev: R. H. C. Davis, EHR, 73, 1958, 142-43; P. E.
   Jones, History, 43, 1958, 134-35.
HEERS, JACQUES. L'Occident aux XIVe et XVe Siècles:
   Aspects Économiques et Sociaux. (Nouvelle Clio: L'His-
   toire et ses Problèmes, 23.) Paris: Presses Universi-
   taires de France, 1963.
HOLMES, G. A. The Estates of the Higher Nobility in
   Fourteenth-Century England. (Cambridge Studies in
   Economic History.) Cambridge and New York: Cambridge
   Univ Press, 1957.
      Rev: T. B. Pugh, History, 43, 1958, 135-37; Sylvia L.
   Thrupp, Spec, 32, 1957, 838-40.
LUNT, WILLIAM E. Financial Relations of the Papacy with
   England 1327-1534. (Studies in Anglo-Papal Relations
   during the Middle Ages, 2.) Cambridge, Mass.: Mediae-
   val Academy of America, 1962.
MISKIMIN, HARRY A. Money, Prices and Foreign Exchange

in Fourteenth-Century France. (Yale Studies in Economics, 15.) New Haven and London: Yale Univ Press, 1963.
   Comparison of money, prices and foreign exchange in England and France during the fourteenth century.
MUNDY, JOHN H., and PETER RIESENBERG. The Mediaeval Town. Princeton, N.J., and London: D. Van Nostrand, 1958. (An Anvil Original, 30.)
POSTAN, M. M., E. E. RICH, and EDWARD MILLER, Eds. The Cambridge Economic History of Europe, III: Economic Organization and Policies in the Middle Ages. Cambridge and New York: Cambridge Univ Press, 1963.
   Extensive bibliography for each of the eight chapters. The first two volumes in this series are listed here in the interest of completeness: Vol. I. The Agrarian Life of the Middle Ages (1941); Vol. II. Trade and Industry in the Middle Ages (1952).
STEEL, ANTHONY. The Receipt of the Exchequer 1377-1485. Cambridge and New York: Cambridge Univ Press, 1954.
   Rev: William E. Lunt, Spec, 30, 1955, 306-8.
TIERNEY, BRIAN. Medieval Poor Law: A Sketch of Canonical Theory and its Application in England. Berkeley: Univ of California Press, 1959.
   Rev: M. D. Knowles, Spec, 35, 1960, 154-56.

RELIGIOUS BACKGROUNDS

See Griffith, pp. 346-55.

BAINTON, ROLAND H. The Medieval Church. Princeton,
N. J.: D. Van Nostrand, 1962. (An Anvil Original.)
Contains (Part I) a short history of western Christi-
anity and (Part II) illustrative documents; select bibliog-
raphy.
Rev: Marshall W. Baldwin, Spec, 39, 1964, 112.
BALDWIN, MARSHALL WHITHED. The Mediaeval Church.
Ithaca, N. Y.: Cornell Univ Press, 1953; London: Oxford
Univ Press, 1954.
BRANDT, WILLIAM J. Church and Society in the Late
Fourteenth Century: A Contemporary View. M and H, 13,
1960, 56-67.
COLLEDGE, ERIC, Ed. The Mediaeval Mystics of England.
New York: Charles Scribner's Sons, 1961.
Rev: Hayden V. White, Spec, 37, 1962, 447-48.
COOK, GEORGE HENRY. The English Mediaeval Parish
Church. London: Phoenix House; New York: Macmillan,
1954.
Rev: TLS, Sept 24, 1954, 604.
----------. English Collegiate Churches of the Middle Ages.
London: Phoenix House, 1959; New York: Macmillan,
1960.

Rev: Nikolaus Pevsner, List, 62, 1959, 994, 997; TLS, Dec 11, 1959, 729.
----------. English Monasteries in the Middle Ages. London: Phoenix House; New York: Macmillan, 1961.
Rev: Dom David Knowles, List, 66, 1961, 213; TLS, Aug 18, 1961, 553; Coburn V. Graves, Spec, 37, 1962, 267-68.
CROSS, F. L., Ed. The Oxford Dictionary of the Christian Church. Oxford: Clarendon Press; New York: Oxford Univ Press, 1957.
Rev: Harry Rosenberg, Spec, 33, 1958, 387-89.
DELHAYE, PHILIPPE. La Philosophie Chrétienne au Moyen Âge. Paris: A. Fayard, 1959. (Je Sais, Je Crois: Encyclopédie du Catholique au XXe Siècle, 12.)
----------. Christian Philosophy in the Middle Ages. Trans. by S. J. Tester. London: Burns and Oates, 1960. (Faith and Fact Books, 12.)
DICKINSON, J. C. Monastic Life in Medieval England. London: A and C Black, 1961; New York: Barnes and Noble, 1962.
Rev: Dom David Knowles, List, 66, 1961, 1082.
FRISTEDT, SVEN L. The Authorship of the Lollard Bible. Summary and Amplification of the Wycliffe Bible, Part I. SMS, 19, 1956, 28-41.
GILSON, ÉTIENNE. History of Christian Philosophy in the Middle Ages. New York: Random House, 1955; London: Sheed and Ward, 1956.
Rev: TLS, Jan 13, 1956, 25; A. S. Godin, Thought, 30, 1956, 460-62.
----------. Elements of Christian Philosophy. Garden City, N.Y.: Doubleday, 1960.
Rev: Leo Sweeney, Spec, 36, 1961, 655-57.
GUILLEMAIN, BERNARD. The Later Middle Ages. Trans. from the French by S. Taylor. London: Burns and Oates; New York: Hawthorn Books, 1960. (Faith and Fact Books, 76.)
HARGREAVES, HENRY. The Middle English Primers and the Wycliffite Bible. MLR, 51, 1956, 215-17.
KING, ARCHDALE A. Liturgies of the Past. London:

Longmans, Green; Milwaukee, Wis.: Bruce Pub. Co.,
1959.
    Rev: TLS, Oct 9, 1959, 580.
KNOWLES, DOM DAVID. The Religious Orders in England,
Vol. II: The End of the Middle Ages. Cambridge and New
York: Cambridge Univ Press, 1955.
    Rev: Richard W. Emery, Spec, 31, 1956, 386-88; List,
55, 1956, 27.
----------. The English Mystical Tradition. London: Burns
and Oates; New York: Harper's, 1961.
    Rev: Francis Wormald, List, 65, 1961, 841-42; John
Lawlor, MLR, 56, 1961, 574-75; Hayden V. White, Spec,
37, 1962, 447-48.
----------. The Monastic Order in England: A History of
its Development from the Times of St. Dunstan to the
Fourth Lateran Council, 940-1216. 2nd ed. Cambridge
and New York: Cambridge Univ Press, 1963.
LECLERCQ, JEAN. L'Amour des Lettres et le Désir de
Dieu: Initiation aux Auteurs Monastiques du Moyen Âge.
Paris: Éditions du Cerf, 1957.
----------. The Love of Learning and the Desire for God:
A Study of Monastic Culture. Trans. from the French by
Catharine Misrahi. New York: Fordham Univ Press, 1961.
    Rev: Giles Constable, Spec, 37, 1962, 138-40.
OWST, G. R. Literature and Pulpit in Medieval England: A
Neglected Chapter in the History of English Letters and of
the English People. 2nd rev. ed. Oxford: Blackwell; New
York: Barnes and Noble, 1961.
    See Griffith, p. 351, for numerous reviews of the 1st
ed. (1933) of this work.
PANTIN, W. A. The English Church in the Fourteenth Century. (Based on the Birbeck Lectures of 1948.) Cambridge
and New York: Cambridge Univ Press, 1955. Reprinted,
with a Foreword to the American Edition by Paul E.
Beichner: Notre Dame, Ind.: Univ of Notre Dame Press,
1963.
    Rev: Claude Jenkins, MAE, 25, 1956, 114-15; TLS, May
6, 1955, p. vii.
PEPLER, CONRAD. The English Religious Heritage. (The

Fourteenth Century Mystics.) London: Blackfriars; St.
Louis, Mo.: Herder, 1958.

PETRY, RAY C., Ed. Late Medieval Mysticism. London:
S. C. M. Press; Philadelphia, Pa.: Westminster Press,
1957. (Library of Christian Classics, 13.)
> Rev: Seyyed Hossein Nasr, Spec, 33, 1958, 430-31.

ROBSON, J. A. Wyclyf and the Oxford Schools: The Relation of the Summa de ente to Scholastic Debates at Oxford
in the later Fourteenth Century. Cambridge and New York:
Cambridge Univ Press, 1961. (Cambridge Studies in
Medieval Life and Thought, 8.)
> Rev: S. Harrison Thomson, Spec, 38, 1963, 497-99.

ROTH, FRANCIS. The English Austin Friars 1249-1538, II:
Sources. New York: Augustinian Historical Institute, 1961.
> Rev: Robert L. Johnson, Jr., Spec, 38, 1963, 659-60.

SITWELL, GERARD. Medieval Spiritual Writers. London:
Burns and Oates, 1961. (Faith and Fact Books.) Ameri-
can ed.: Spiritual Writers of the Middle Ages. New York:
Hawthorn Books, 1961.

SMALLEY, BERYL. English Friars and Antiquity in the
Early Fourteenth Century. Oxford: Blackwell, 1960; New
York: Barnes and Noble, 1961.
> Rev: John R. Williams, Spec, 37, 1962, 307-11; Denys
Hay, EHR, 77, 1962, 530-32.

TIERNEY, BRIAN. Medieval Poor Law: A Sketch of Canonical Theory and its Application in England. Berkeley: Univ
of California Press, 1959.
> Rev: M. D. Knowles, Spec, 35, 1960, 154-56.

UENO, NAOZO. The Religious View of Chaucer in His
Italian Period. Tokyo: Nanundo, 1958.

SCIENTIFIC BACKGROUNDS

See Griffith, pp. 356-62.

Note: Contributions to the history of mediaeval science have been so numerous during the past decade, and the field itself is so broad, that no attempt can be made in a Bibliography of this nature to provide the reader with a systematic survey of the subject. Accordingly, entries in this section have been limited to (a) bibliographical resources, (b) general works in the history of science, and (c) studies which are directly related to Chaucer's scientific knowledge. In the interest of comprehensiveness, mention should be made here of two bibliographical guides which were published earlier than the terminus a quo of this bibliography; neither is listed in Griffith: H. Guerlac, Science in Western Civilization: A Syllabus (New York: 1952); George Sarton, A Guide to the History of Science, with Introductory Essays on Science and Tradition (Waltham, Mass.: 1952).

AIKEN, PAULINE. Vincent of Beauvais and the "Houres" of Chaucer's Physician. SP, 53, 1956, 22-24.
AMERICAN GEOGRAPHICAL SOCIETY. Research Catalogue. 15 vols. Boston: G. K. Hall, 1962.
Information of interest to the mediaevalist is found in Vol. II of this bibliography, under the following "General

Topical Numbers:" 65. Geographical Knowledge of Moslems and Other Oriental Peoples (600 A. D. -1800 A. D.); 66. Geographical Knowledge of Western Europeans and Christians (150 A. D. -1300 A. D. Includes Christians of the Near East); 67. Geographical Knowledge of Western Europeans and Christians (1300 A. D. -1600 A. D.); also a few references are to be found under Topic No. 94: History: 750-1500.

ARCHIVES INTERNATIONALES D'HISTOIRE DES SCIENCES. Revue trimestrielle publiée par la Division d'Histoire des Sciences de l'Union Internationale d'Histoire et de Philosophie des Sciences et avec le Concours Financier de l'UNESCO. Paris.
    Supersedes Archeion. A "Bibliographie Critique" is included in each issue.

ARTELT, W. Index zur Geschichte der Medizin, Naturwissenschaft und Technik. Munich and Berlin, Vol. I (1953)--.

THE BRITISH JOURNAL FOR THE HISTORY OF SCIENCE. Published by the British Society for the History of Science (London). Vol. I (Parts I-IV), 1962-63--.
    Numerous reviews; a useful check-list entitled "Titles of Papers in Current Periodicals on the History of Science" is included in each issue.

BÜHLER, CURT F. A Middle English Medical Manuscript from Norwich. Pp. 285-98 in Studies in Medieval Literature: In Honor of Professor Albert Croll Baugh, edited by MacEdward Leach. Philadelphia: Univ of Pennsylvania Press; London: Oxford Univ Press, 1961.

BULLOUGH, VERN L. Duke Humphrey and His Medical Collections. Revue Nouvelle, 14, 1961, 87-91.

----------. Medical Study at Mediaeval Oxford. Spec, 36, 1961, 600-12.

CARMODY, FRANCIS J. Arabic Astronomical and Astrological Sciences in Latin Translation: A Critical Bibliography. Berkeley: Univ of California Press, 1956.
    Rev: E. S. Kennedy, Spec, 32, 1957, 339-41.

CLAGETT, MARSHALL. The Science of Mechanics in the Middle Ages. (Univ of Wisconsin Publications in Medieval

Science, 4.) Madison, Wisconsin; London: Oxford Univ
Press, 1959.
> Rev: C. Truesdell, Spec, 36, 1961, 119-21.

CROMBIE, A. C. Medieval and Early Modern Science,
Vol. I: Science in the Middle Ages: V-XIII Centuries;
Vol. II: Science in the Later Middle Ages and Early Modern Times: XIII- XVII Centuries. Garden City, N.Y.:
Doubleday and Co., 1959. (Anchor Book, A 167 a/b.)
> Revision, in 2 vols., of the author's Augustine to Gal-
ileo: The History of Science A.D. 400-1600. London: Fal-
con Press, 1952; Cambridge, Mass.: Harvard Univ Press,
1953. Rev. ed., 1959. Extensive analytical bibliography.

----------, Ed. Scientific Change:Historical Studies in the
Intellectual, Social and Technical Conditions for Scientific
Discovery and Technical Invention, from Antiquity to the
Present: Symposium on the History of Science, Univ of
Oxford 9-15 July 1961. Part III: Science and Technology in
the Middle Ages. New York: Basic Books, 1963.

CURRENT WORK IN THE HISTORY OF MEDICINE. London:
Wellcome Historical Medical Library. Vol. I, 1954--.
> Quarterly bibliography.

CURRY, WALTER CLYDE. Chaucer and the Mediaeval Sciences. 2nd rev. ed. New York: Barnes and Noble; London:
Allen and Unwin, 1960. Paper reprint: Barnes and Noble,
1962.
> See Griffith, p. 357, for reviews of the 1st ed.
> Rev: Lynn Thorndike, Spec, 35, 1960, 445; Thomas Jay
Garbaty, BA, 35, 1961, 285.

DAUMAS, MAURICE, et al., Eds. Histoire de la Science.
(Encyclopédie de la Pléiade.) Paris: Gallimard, 1957.
> Rev: G. Canguilhem, Archives Internationales d'His-
toire des Sciences, 49, 1959, 76-82.

----------, Ed. Histoire Générale des Techniques, Vol. I:
Les Origines de la Civilisation Technique. Paris: Presses
Universitaires de France, 1962.
> This volume, the first of four projected, brings the
subject down to about 1350.

DERRY, T. K., and TREVOR I. WILLIAMS. A Short History of Technology from the Earliest Times to A.D. 1900.

Oxford: Clarendon Press, 1960; New York: Oxford Univ
Press, 1961.
Rev: Robert S. Woodbury, Spec, 37, 1962, 270-71;
Thomas P. Hughes, Isis, 54, 1963, 417-18.
GORDON, BENJAMIN LEE. Medieval and Renaissance
Medicine. New York: Philosophical Library, 1959.
Rev: Loren MacKinney, Spec, 35, 1960, 605-7.
GRENNEN, JOSEPH EDWARD. Jargon Transmuted: Alchemy
in Chaucer's Canon's Yeoman's Tale. DA, 22, 859. Ford-
ham Univ, 1960.
See also the two articles by Grennen under CYT.
HASKINS, C. H. Studies in the History of Mediaeval Sci-
ence. 2nd ed. (1927) reprinted. New York: Frederick
Ungar; London: Constable, 1961.
See Griffith, p. 358, for notice and reviews of 1st ed.
HERTZ, JOHN ATLEE. Chapters Toward a Study of Chau-
cer's Knowledge of Geography. DA, 19, 2600-1. Lehigh
Univ, 1959.
HOLMYARD, E. J. Alchemy. Harmondsworth, England,
and Baltimore, Md.: Penguin Books, 1957.
ISIS: An International Review Devoted to the History of Sci-
ence and its Cultural Influences. Official Quarterly Jour-
nal of the History of Science Society. Baltimore, Md.:
The Johns Hopkins Univ.
Annual critical bibliography and numerous reviews.
MEDICAL HISTORY. Official Organ of the Cambridge Uni-
versity History of Medicine Society, the Norwegian Soci-
ety for the History of Medicine, the Scottish Society of the
History of Medicine, and the Osler Club of London. Lon-
don: Vol. I, 1957--.
Numerous reviews.
MORTON, LESLIE T. Garrison and Morton's Medical Bib-
liography: An Annotated Check-List of Texts Illustrating
the History of Medicine. 2nd rev. ed. London: Grafton
and Co., 1954.
Items 6376-6703 (pp. 558-81) illustrate the History of
Medicine.
O'CONNOR, JOHN J. The Astrological Background of the
Miller's Tale. Spec, 31, 1956, 120-25.

----------. The Astronomical Dating of Chaucer's Troilus.
JEGP, 55, 1956, 556-62.
PALTER, ROBERT M. , Ed. Toward Modern Science, I:
Studies in Ancient and Medieval Science; II: Studies in
Renaissance Science. New York: Farrar, Straus, and
Cudahy (Noonday Press), 1961.
Rev: Edward Grant, Spec, 37, 1962, 291-93.
PRICE, DEREK J. The Equatorie of the Planetis. With a
Linguistic Analysis by R. M. Wilson. Cambridge Univ
Press, 1955.
See section Editions with Notes for reviews.
RUSSO, FRANÇOIS. Histoire des Sciences et des Tech-
niques: Bibliographie. (Actualités Scientifiques et Indus-
trielles, 1204.) Paris: Hermann, 1954.
SINGER, CHARLES, E. J. HOLMYARD, A. R. HALL, and
TREVOR I. WILLIAMS, Eds. A History of Technology,
II: The Mediterranean Civilizations and the Middle Ages,
c. 700 B. C. to c. A. D. 1500. Oxford: Clarendon Press;
New York: Oxford Univ Press, 1956.
Rev: An entire issue of Technology and Culture (Vol. I,
No. 4, Fall, 1960) is devoted to review of the five volumes
of this work. The review of central interest to mediaeval-
ists is by Lynn White , Jr. , pp. 339-44.
SINGER, CHARLES. A Short History of Scientific Ideas to
1900. Oxford: Clarendon Press; New York: Oxford Univ
Press, 1959.
Rev: Marshall Clagett, Spec, 36, 1961, 352-53.
----------, and E. ASHWORTH UNDERWOOD. A Short
History of Medicine. 2nd rev. ed. Oxford: Clarendon
Press; New York: Oxford Univ Press, 1962.
STEADMAN, JOHN M. Chauntecleer and Medieval Natural
History. Isis, 50, 1959, 236-44.
TATON, RENÉ, General Ed. Histoire générale des Sci-
ences, I: La Science Antique et Médiévale (des Origines
à 1450), par R. Arnaldez et al. Paris: Presses Universi-
taires de France, 1957--.
Bibliography at the end of each chapter.
----------. Trans. into English by A. J. Pomerans. New
York: Basic Books, 1963.
TECHNOLOGY AND CULTURE. The International Quarterly

of the Society for the History of Technology. Detroit,
Mich.: Wayne State Univ Press, Vol. I, 1959--.

In addition to numerous book reviews and bibliographical notes, this journal has recently (Vol. I, Winter, 1964)
instituted an annual bibliography of current works in the
history of technology. The first of these bibliographies
includes 171 items published during 1962.

VAN CITTERT, P. H. Astrolabes: A Critical Description of
the Astrolabes, Noctilabes and Quadrants in the Care of
the Utrecht University Museum. Leiden, Netherlands,
1954.

Rev: E. S. Kennedy, Spec, 31, 1956, 209.

WHITE, BEATRICE. Medieval Animal Lore. Ang, 72, 1954,
21-30.

The subject of this paper (originally read at the International Conference of University Professors of English,
Paris, August, 1963) is the tradition of the Physiologus
in the Middle Ages. Reference to Chaucer's NPT.

WHITE, LYNN, JR. Medieval Technology and Social Change.
Oxford: Clarendon Press; New York: Oxford Univ Press,
1962.

Rev: John Hale, Spect, March 16, 1962, 340; Marshall Clagett, Spec, 39, 1964, 359-65; Joseph Needham,
Isis, 54, 1963, 418-20; Joseph R. Strayer, Technology
and Culture, 4, 1963, 62-65.

ARTISTIC BACKGROUNDS

See Griffith, pp. 363-68.

ANDERSON, M. D. Misericords. Medieval Life in English Woodcarving. Harmondsworth, England, and Baltimore, Md.: Penguin Books, 1954.
> Rev: TLS, Feb 25, 1955, 116.

APEL, WILLI. The Notation of Polyphonic Music, 900-1600. 5th rev. ed. Cambridge, Mass.: The Mediaeval Academy of America, 1961.
> See Griffith, p. 363, for notice of 1st ed.

APFEL, ERNST. Studien zur Satztechnik der Mittelalterlichen englischen Musik. Part I: Text; Part II: Transcriptions. (Abhandlungen der Heidelberger Akademie der Wissenschaften.) Heidelberg: C. Winter, 1959.
> Rev: Luther A. Dittmer, Spec, 36, 1961, 443-47.

ARNOLD, HUGH. Stained Glass of the Middle Ages in England and France. With fifty Plates in Color by Lawrence B. Saint. New York: Macmillan, 1955.
> Reprint of the 2nd ed. (1939); see Griffith, p. 363, for notice of reprint of 1st ed. (1913).

BALTRUŠAITIS, JURGIS. Le Moyen Âge Fantastique: Antiquités et Exotismes dans l'Art Gothique. (Collection Henri Focillon, 3.) Paris: Armand Colin, 1955.
> Rev: George Levitine, Spec, 33, 1958, 77-79.

BEICHNER, PAUL E. The Medieval Representative of

Music, Jubal or Tubalcain? (Texts and Studies in the
History of Medieval Education, 2.) Notre Dame, Ind.:
Univ of Notre Dame Press, 1954.
References to BD.
BOASE, T. S. R. English Illumination of the 13th and 14th
Centuries. Oxford: Bodleian Library, 1954.
CARTER, HENRY HOLLAND. A Dictionary of Middle Eng-
lish Musical Terms. Edited by George B. Gerhard and
Others. (Indiana Univ Humanities Series, 45.) Blooming-
ton, Ind.: Indiana Univ Press, 1961.
Bibliography, pp. 569-649.
CHYDENIUS, JOHN. The Theory of Medieval Symbolism.
(Societas Scientiarum Fennica. Commentationes human-
arum litterarum, 27, 2.) Helsinki: Academic Bookstore;
Copenhagen: Munksgaard, 1960.
COLVERT, JAMES B. A Reference to Music in Chaucer's
House of Fame. MLN, 69, 1954, 239-41.
HF, 696.
DELAISSE, L. M. J. La Miniature en Angleterre à la Fin
du XIVe Siècle. Script, 1954, pp. 128-35.
DUPONT, JACQUES, and CESARE GRUDI. Gothic Painting.
Trans. by Stuart Gilbert. New York: Skira; London:
Zwemmer; Toronto: Burns and MacEachern, 1954.
Rev: TLS, Feb 11, 1955, 86.
FITCHEN, JOHN. The Construction of Gothic Cathedrals:
A Study of Medieval Vault Erection. Oxford: Clarendon
Press; New York: Oxford Univ Press, 1961.
Rev: Carl D. Sheppard, Jr., Spec, 36, 1961, 651-52.
FRANKL, PAUL. The Gothic: Literary Sources and Inter-
pretations through Eight Centuries. Princeton, N.J.:
Princeton Univ Press, 1960.
Rev: Wolfgang Stechow, Spec, 37, 1962, 123-26.
GROUT, DONALD J. A History of Western Music. New
York: Norton, 1960.
Bibliography, pp. 668-94.
HARMAN, ALEC. Mediaeval and Early Renaissance Music.
Fairlawn, N.J.: Essential Books; London: Rockliff, 1958.
Rev: Lincoln Bunce Spiess, Spec, 35, 1960, 116-18.
HARRISON, FRANK LL. Music in Medieval Britain. Edited

by Egon Wellesz. London: Routledge and Kegan Paul,
1958; New York: Praeger, 1959.

HARVEY, JOHN. English Mediaeval Architects: A Biographical Dictionary down to 1550 Including Master Masons,
Carpenters, Carvers, Building Contractors and Others
Responsible for Design. London: Batsford; Boston: Boston Book and Art Shop, 1954.

Rev: List, 53, 1955, 629; R. Furneaux Jordan, Obs,
Jan 16, 1955, 9; TLS, March 11, 1955, 152; Kenneth John
Conant, Spec, 33, 1958, 92-93.

HUGHES, DOM ANSELM, Ed. The New Oxford History of
Music. Vol. II: Early Medieval Music up to 1300. London
and New York: Oxford Univ Press, 1954.

----------, and GERALD ABRAHAM. Vol. III: Ars Nova
and the Renaissance, 1300-1540. London and New York:
Oxford Univ Press, 1960.

LADENDORF, H. Antikenstudium und Antikenkopie: Vorar-
beiten zu einer Darstellung ihrer Bedeutung in der mittelalterlichen und neueren Zeit. (Abhandlungen der Säch-
sischen Akademie der Wissenschaften zu Leipzig.) 2nd
enlarged ed. Berlin: Akademie Verlag, 1958.

MORGAN, B. G. Canonic Design in English Mediaeval
Architecture: the Origins and Nature of Systematic Archi-
tectural Design in England, 1215-1515. Liverpool: Univ
Press, 1961.

MROCZKOWSKI, PRZEMYSLAW. Mediaeval Art and Aesthetics in The Canterbury Tales. Spec, 33, 1958, 204-21.

OAKESHOTT, WALTER. Classical Inspiration in Medieval
Art. (Rhind Lectures in Archaeology, 1956.) London:
Chapman and Hall, 1959; New York: Praeger, 1960.

Rev: J. E. Gaehde, Spec, 36, 1961, 678-82.

PÄCHT, OTTO. The Rise of Pictorial Narrative in Twelfth-
century England. Oxford: Clarendon Press, 1962.

PANOFSKY, ERWIN. Renaissance and Renascences in Western Art. (The Gottesman Lectures, Uppsala Univ, 7.)
Copenhagen: Russak; Stockholm: Almqvist and Wiksell,
1960.

Bibliography, pp. 211-30.

----------. Gothic Architecture and Scholasticism. New
York: Meridian Books, 1957.

Paperback reprint of the 1st ed. (1951).

PARRISH, CARL. The Notation of Mediaeval Music. London: Faber and Faber; New York: Norton, 1957. 2nd rev. ed., 1959.

RICKERT, MARGARET. Painting in Britain. The Middle Ages. (Pelican History of Art.) Harmondsworth, England, and Baltimore, Md.: Penguin Books, 1954.

Rev: List, 53, 1955, 393; TLS, Feb 4, 1955, 68.

ROBERTSON, ALEC, and DENIS STEVENS. The Pelican History of Music. I: Ancient Forms to Polyphony. Harmondsworth, England, and•Baltimore, Md.: Penguin Books, 1960.

Bibliography, pp. 323-26; discography, pp. 327-31.

SCHRADE, LEO. Polyphonic Music of the Fourteenth Century. I: The Roman de Fauvel; The Works of Philippe de Vitry; French Cycles of the Ordinarium Missae. II-III: The Works of Guillaume de Machaut. Separate commentary to each volume. Les Ramparts, Monaco: Editions de L'Oiseau-Lyre, 1956.

Rev: Willi Apel, Spec, 32, 1957, 863-66 (for Vol. I); ibid., 33, 1958, 433-44 (for Vols. II-III).

SIMSON, OTTO VON. The Gothic Cathedral: Origins of Gothic Architecture and the Mediaeval Concept of Order. With an Appendix on the Proportions of the South Tower of Chartres Cathedral by Ernest Levy. New York: Pub. for Bollingen Foundation by Pantheon Books, 1956. (Bollingen Series, 48.) 2nd rev. ed., 1962.

Rev: Kenneth John Conant, Spec, 33, 1958, 154-58.

SMITH, E. BALDWIN. Architectural Symbolism of Imperial Rome and the Middle Ages. (Princeton Monographs in Art and Archaeology, 30.) Princeton, N.J.: Princeton Univ Press, 1956.

Rev: Kenneth John Conant, Spec, 33, 1958, 137-39.

STONE, LAWRENCE. Sculpture in Britain. The Middle Ages. (The Pelican History of Art.) Harmondsworth, England, and Baltimore, Md.: Penguin Books, 1955.

Rev: Francis Wormald, List, 54, 1955, 710; TLS, Aug 19, 1955, 474.

TRISTRAM, E. W. English Wall Painting of the Fourteenth Century. Edited by Eileen Tristram, with a Catalogue by

E. W. Tristram. Compiled in Collaboration with Monica
Bardswell. London: Routledge and Kegan Paul, 1955.
   Rev: TLS, May 20, 1955, 264.
WEBB, GEOFFREY. Architecture in Britain. The Middle
Ages. (The Pelican History of Art.) Harmondsworth,
England, and Baltimore, Md.: Penguin Books, 1956.
   Rev: Peter Kidson, List, 56, 1956, 956.

CONCORDANCE AND INDEXES

See Griffith, pp. 3-4.

MAGOUN, FRANCIS P., JR. A Chaucer Gazetteer. Chicago: Univ of Chicago Press, 1961.
  For reviews, see section General Criticism.
TATLOCK, J. S. P., and ARTHUR G. KENNEDY. A Concordance to the Complete Works of Geoffrey Chaucer and to the Romaunt of the Rose. Reprint. Gloucester, Mass.: Peter Smith, 1963.
  See Griffith, pp. 3-4, for description and reviews of this concordance; first published in 1927.

INDEX

Individual works by Chaucer are listed alphabetically by title in this index. The <u>Canterbury Tales</u> has been fully indexed: each tale within the collection is separately listed in the index, as are individual Canterbury pilgrims. Other literary works are entered under the name of the author; if the author's name is unknown, the work is listed by title. Names of reviewers have not ordinarily been indexed. Reviews which approach article length, however, or reviews which contribute to a controversy, are entered under the name of the reviewer.